reception room, study, guest room, childrens bedroom, and toilet in north/northwest

main entrance, office/study, basement below, valuables storage, and reception hall/lounge

prayer/meditatiion, basement below, living room, and children's bedroom

childrens b... study, livin... storage, a... dining roo...

main entrance, ...room, ...ce, and ...below

kitchen, central heating, and electircal equipment

...yer/meditatiion, ...ement below, ...g room, and ...dren's bedroom

childrens bedroom, study, living room, storage, and dining room

free space for the

auspicious inside positioning

ether element

main entrance, reception room, study/office, bathroom, and basement below

adults bedroom, heavy storage, and recreation

staircase, bedroom, and heavy storage

...entral ...heating, and electircal equipment

...ning

...ain entrance, ...ception room, ...tudy/office, ...athroom, and ...asement below

adults bedroom, heavy storage, and recreation

dining room, staircase, bedroom, and heavy storage

kitchen, central heating, and electircal equipment

reception room, study, guest room, childrens bedroom, and toilet in north/northwest

main entrance, office/study, basement below, valuables storage, and reception hall/lounge

prayer/meditatiion, basement below, living room, and children's bedroom

...tchen, central ...eating, and ...ectircal ...quipment

reception room, study, guest room, childrens bedroom, and toilet in north/northwest

main entrance, office/study, basement below, valuables storage, and reception hall/lounge

prayer/meditatiion, basement below, living room, and children's bedroom

childrens bedroom, study, living room, storage, and dining room

free space for the

auspicious inside positioning

ether element

main entrance, reception room, study/office, bathroom, and basement below

...yer/meditatiion, ...ement below, ...g room, and ...dren's bedroom

childrens bedroom, study, living room, storage, and dining room

free space for the

auspicious inside positioning

ether element

main entrance, reception room, study/office, bathroom, and basement below

adults bedroom, heavy storage, and recreation

dining room, staircase, bedroom, and heavy storage

kitchen, central heating, and electircal equipment

...ning

...ain entrance, ...ception room, ...udy/office, ...athroom, and ...asement below

adults bedroom, heavy storage, and recreation

dining room, staircase, bedroom, and heavy storage

kitchen, central heating, and electircal equipment

reception room, study, guest room, childrens bedroom, and toilet in north/northwest

main entrance, office/study, basement below, valuables storage, and reception hall/lounge

prayer/meditatiio... basement below, living room, and children's bedroo...

...tchen, central ...eating, and ...ectircal ...quipment

reception room, study, guest room, childrens bedroom, and toilet in north/northwest

main entrance, office/study, basement below, valuables storage, and reception hall/lounge

prayer/meditatiion, basement below, living room, and children's bedroom

childrens bedroom, study, living room, storage, and dining room

free space for the

auspicious inside positioning

ether element

main entrance, reception room study/office, bathroom, and basement below

...yer/meditatiion, ...ement below, ...g room, and ...dren's bedroom

childrens bedroom, study, living room, storage, and dining room

free space for the

auspicious inside positioning

ether element

main entrance, reception room, study/office, bathroom, and basement below

adults bedroom, heavy storage, and recreation

dining room, staircase, bedroom, and heavy storage

kitchen, central heating, and electircal equipment

...ning

...ain entrance, ...ception room, ...udy/office, ...throom, and ...sement below

adults bedroom, heavy storage, and recreation

dining room, staircase, bedroom, and heavy storage

kitchen, central heating, and electircal equipment

reception room, study, guest room, childrens bedroom, and toilet in north/northwest

main entrance, office/study, basement below, valuables storage, and reception hall/lounge

prayer/meditatiio... basement below, living room, and children's bedroo...

VASTU
The Origin of
FENG SHUI

**Energize Your Home and Office
With Nature's Heavenly Influences**

Marcus Schmieke

Dedicated to all those who respect Nature and our surrounding environment.

Acknowledgments:
Shalil Bhattessa; K. Jegeswaran; Nimai Smith - photography and design
consultant; Brendan Greene - proofreading; Donna Warman - proofreading;
Allan Fong - design consultant; Subramaniam Wichweswaran.

First published in Great Britain

British Library Cataloguing-in-Publication Data.
A catalogue record for this book is available from the British Library.

ISBN No. 0 9527 5801 6

Printed in Singapore

GOLOKA
BOOKS

Back cover picture: The world famous Taj Mahal in Agra, India,
built according to the principles of *Vastu*.

Contents - Level One

Contents - Level Two

Contents - Level Two

Contents - Level Two

Foreword

Have you ever walked into a building or house and thought, 'The vibes in this place are wonderful, breathtaking, amazing!'? Or to the contrary, "My God, I don't like the vibes in this place!"? On both counts, we've all had such positive and negative feelings about a room, house, building, forest, or park at one time or another. Additionally, we've had similar feelings about the good, bad, or mixed vibes or energies we get from people.

But what exactly are these 'vibes' or 'energies' that emanate from people and buildings? When a particular place makes you feel uneasy or even ill while other places make you feel good and healthy, this is a real effect with a real cause. So Nature's good and bad energies are just as real as the effects on your body and mind.

The whole science of *Vastu* is the art of positioning your home and office to attract Nature's auspicious influences and to block Her inauspicious influences. It is as simple as that, but sometimes it becomes rather more complicated to implement. How Nature's subtle forces profoundly influence everyone at every moment is often overlooked. Unveiling the reality of Nature's multifarious influences is the agenda of this book, and how to harmonise those influences is the ancient solution given by *Vastu*.

An acute awareness of Nature's subtle yet powerful influences that are constantly entering everyone's immediate surroundings is concisely presented. How positive and negative energies come from the eight directions and how they affect you and your house is clearly revealed. *Vastu* is based upon scientific energetic principles expounded in the oldest writings in the world. Check out Nature's energies that you are 'living with', open up your living spaces to Her auspicious influences, block all Her negative energies, and experience a significant improvement right in your own office or home. Om tat sat.

Arthur Smith
(Certified *Vastu*/Vasati consultant, editor, and contributing author)

Introduction

Visit any antiquated architectural monument anywhere in the world and you'll experience a distinct sensation of energy and harmony. Enter ancient buildings like Andrea Palladio´s famous Florentine villas and you'll feel a profound well-being unknown within the walls of contemporary Western buildings. The secret is that those masters of yore knew how to build structures in precise harmony with Nature's universal laws. These same laws are fundamental to the architectural style of the Chinese Feng Shui, European geomancy, and the old Mesoamerican people called the Maya, to name a few. But India's *Vastu* scriptures, dating from around 5,000 years ago, carry the earliest known architectural disciplines of Nature's universal laws.

Archaeological excavations of pre-historic sites belonging to highly developed cultures all over the Earth have consistently revealed that the living and building arrangements of our far distant ancestors were constructed in accordance with Nature's gross and subtle influences. Protecting and enhancing wealth, health, and prosperity were clearly their aims. The further back in history we go the more we see that various cultures shared very similar values, particularly the finer knowledge of building and living in harmony with Nature. The most visible preservation of the ancient art of building and living is found in Far Eastern countries like China and India. And today we see a worldwide revival of that art of building and living.

Those buildings that have withstood millenniums of natural disasters are mainly those that were built according to *Vastu* principles, as verified by India's oldest structures. Hardly any other architectural tradition has structures that have lasted 5,000 years and are still being used today. Nowadays, the ancient subtle concepts of congenial living are virtually non-existent in general building culture.

Interestingly enough, the renowned Roman architect Vitruvius was acquainted with India's *Vastu* scriptures. The evidence lies in the chapters of his legendary *opus De re architectura* which exactly match the chapter sequence in the *Manasara*, a classic *Vastu* scripture. Vitruvius lived 2,000 years ago. His work inspired Andrea Palladio, who incorporated *Vastu* principles in the world-famous 16th century Renaissance Architecture. The secret knowledge behind this work and the origin of his architecture has recently been revealed. Within these pages you'll discover not only the essential secret sources of that knowledge but empowerment to transform the quality of your living and working spaces.

Marcus Schmieke

Origin of Vastu

The great science of *Vastu*, the art of building your home in harmony with Nature's laws, originated in India. *Vastu* is part of the *Stapatya Veda* that comes from the *Atharva Veda* which is one of the four *Vedas*. The *Vedas* are the oldest writings on India's ancient history, science, philosophy, and culture. Five thousand years ago, the great sage Srila Vyasadeva compiled the four *Vedas* which contain millions of verses.

The word 'Veda' means complete knowledge, and the original *Veda* is said to have been spoken by God at the time of the material creation trillions of years ago. According to Vedic world history, prior to 5,000 years ago, books were not required: the memories of the people were so powerful that they could remember all they had heard throughout most of their lives. The brilliant sages throughout the ages would teach the unwritten *Veda* to their disciples, and in this way the *Veda* descended through numerous generations in tact. This system of preserving ancient knowledge is called *parampara*, or disciplic succession. Books became a necessity at the dawning of the Iron Age 5,000 years ago when peoples' memories began to rapidly deteriorate. The massive *Veda* was far too difficult for people to remember or even comprehend, so the *Vedas* were compiled for this age.

The essence of the *Vedas* teaches of the human need for spiritual development. Many parts of the *Vedas* additionally teach us how to improve ourselves materially in order to make spiritual progress easier. A few examples are the *Gandharva-veda*, containing the ancient Indian science of music; the *Ayurveda*, depicting medical knowledge; the *Dhanur-veda*, presenting the military science of weapons and warfare; the *Jyostisha-veda*, providing astronomy and astrology; and the *Stapatya-veda* and other such scriptures also referred to as the *Vastu-sastras* which expound the ancient art of constructing buildings auspiciously — in harmony with Nature.

The science of *Vastu* originated when Lord Brahma, a demigod empowered by God to create, was creating a multitude of auspicious and inauspicious beings at the beginning of the creation. While so engaged, Lord Brahma and the demigods attempted to create the 'aura', but instead a formless demon named Vastu Purush appeared. He was the manifestation of unrestrained chaotic energy. This demon needed to be contained since he was threatening to wreak havoc throughout the universe. Lord Brahma and the demigods devised a plan to stop him. They threw him to Earth and sat on him. Being pinned down in this way, with Lord Brahma in the middle and many exalted demigods and sages surrounding him, the Vastu Purush was completely purified and thereafter was celebrated as a *mahabhagavata*, a great devotee of God. This is confirmed by the ancient Vedic mantra: *om mahabhagavataya vastupurushaya svaha*.

The purified Vastu Purush thereafter surrendered himself to Lord Brahma, and said, "My Lord, how can I serve you?" Lord Brahma replied, "I want you to stay here on Earth and be the Lord in all houses and buildings."

After agreeing to serve Lord Brahma, the Vastu Purush inquired: "In the Satya (golden), Treta (silver), and Dvarpara (bronze) *yugas* (ages), people will build

Vastu (pronounced with a short a) in Sanskrit means 'Nature and surrounding environment'. The word Vaastu (with a long a) refers to all types of buildings.

Applying Vastu to living and working structures not only gives protection from subtle negative influences but attracts auspicious energies to help maintain and increase one's health, prosperity, and wisdom.

Lord Brahma, the powerful four-headed sub creator of our universe. The centre of all buildings should be reserved for his auspicious presence.

VASTU - The Origin of Feng Shui

The Vedas teach that we are eternal living entities and have taken temporary bodies. Both the body and the house are our temporary temples, therefore we should utilise our time in this sphere to attain the eternal realm where everything is completely auspicious.

Ancient Indian temples reflect our multidimensional universe according to cosmic laws. They connect us with Nature's higher beings and harmonious universal forces.

India's ancient times are described as extremely prosperous. In particular the architects of the greatest structures drew their plans based entirely upon the laws of Vastu. Aristocrats would never buy plots or buildings that contravened Vastu.

their houses according to *Vastu* and will offer loving services to God, Lord Vishnu, and I will enjoy a share of those offerings. But in the Kali-yuga (the age we are in now), people will build houses in which I will suffer (with bad Vastu) and they will not offer any services to my master Lord Vishnu, or God. Nor will they offer me any food which has been offered to Lord Vishnu. What shall I do and what will I eat?" Lord Brahma replied: "If people in the Kali-yuga cramp you into inauspiciously built buildings and neglect to offer God food which you will enjoy, then you may eat them." How the Vastu Purush does this within dwellings, and how you can appease him, is all explained herein. Later, a disciple of Lord Brahma named Maya Danava founded the science of *Vastuvidya* which is still prominent throughout North India today.

The inside and outside area of every building is portrayed in a Vastu Purush Mandala grid that contains 81 different energy fields (see page 105). In the centre is the *brahma-sthan*, the place where Lord Brahma resides. In the fields surrounding Lord Brahma reside many other great demigods and sages who are all positioned on various parts of the Vastu Purush's body. In the northeast of all buildings lies the head of the Vastu Purush and it is therefore very inauspicious to have a toilet in the northeast. Later chapters in this book explain the consequences of various serious Vastu defects, as well as the rewards of having good Vastu, and most importantly how Vastu defects can easily be corrected.

Compared to Feng Shui, which is considered to be around 3,000 years old, *Vastu*'s written history is at least 5,000 years old. 'Living witnesses' of *Vastu*'s age are the 5,500-year-old cities of the Indus-Sarasvati Culture in India which were discovered in 1921. The first city was found near the village Harappa, and hence their culture became known as the Harappa Civilisation.

One well-known city from this era is Mohenjo-Daro. This city was planned in a grid system with streets going perpendicularly from north to south and from west to east, dividing the city into rectangular blocks. The houses of Mohenjo-Daro were built with their square or rectangular sides facing the main directions, and each house possessed a central courtyard. These features are found in every city of the Harappa civilisation. All their cities were planned like chess boards and were divided into squares of like dimensions, purposely forming various city areas with different functions. The temple was always placed in the city centre.

It is no coincidence that every detail in all those cities conforms to strict *Vastu* principles. The cities did not grow organically but were planned systematically, following clear geometrical *Vastu* concepts. All these facts prove irrefutably that the science of *Vastu* existed even before the 5,500-year-old Harappa cities were constructed.

Few are aware of *Vastu*'s previous application in the Western hemisphere, dating back to the famous Roman architect Marcus Vitruvius. The energetic codes known to European geomancy and its modern scientific traditions over the last few hundred years (Viktor Schauberger, Wilhelm Reich, von Reichenbach) also correspond to *Vastu* principles. This verifies that *Vastu* principles were applied in Western countries in the past and are therefore just as rel-

Origin of Vastu

evant in the present. According to authoritative sources of Vedic history, Greece and Italy were controlled by King Pariksit from Hastinapur (now Delhi) 5,000 years ago. Verification of this can be found in the precise *Vastu* architecture found in the ancient ruins of both these cities.

We are living in an era where our activities are thoughtlessly dominated by economic and pragmatic decisions. Most of us live without any consideration for Nature's inescapable subtle laws that constantly and exactingly reward and punish us at every moment. Even a thousand years ago it was customary to build houses according to natural principles of harmony, the same principles Western countries are now adopting from China and India. Humankind over the last century has tried to violate Nature's laws like never before, celebrating ourselves as the centre of the universe, as if we were more powerful than God. Now, Nature's laws are beginning to severely reprimand our past mistakes in the form of global warming and many unnatural diseases and disturbances. But there is hope, there is a current growing worldwide trend of concern for the environment. The increasing interest in *Vastu* and Feng Shui demonstrates that the more sensitive and sensible sectors of human society want to re-establish harmonious connections with Nature.

According to Vedic texts, the world 5,000 years ago didn't have anywhere near the amount of diseases and problems that we face today. Without machines and endless pollution, they built beautiful houses and cities that were auspicious places to live in, all according to the science of *Vastu*, the ancient Vedic art of living in perfect harmony with Nature.

The science of Vastu is part of the Stapatya Veda which is part of the Atharva Veda. The latter is regarded as one of the four Vedas which taken together comprise many thousands of volumes. The four Vedas consist of philosophical treatises called Upanishads and are educational discourses between the Vedic sages (rishis) and their disciples.

Origin of Feng Shui

The original Lord Buddha

Building in India depicting erotic sculptures

Over the last few thousand years, the Chinese have imbibed some of India's Vedic culture, particularly the great science of *Vastu*, otherwise known in China as Feng Shui. Chinese traditions and culture go back around 3,000 years while India's Vedic culture extends as far back in recorded history as 5,500 years. Although India and China are separated by the huge Himalayan mountains, Vedic culture nevertheless entered China, and the following are some prime evidences:

1. Buddhism originated in India around 3,500 years ago. But Buddhism in India lasted only 1,000 years until it was almost entirely driven out of India by the powerful Sankacharya. (The essential history is that out of compassion for the innocent animals who were being uncharacteristically slaughtered for meat consumption, Lord Buddha descended and controversially taught everyone to reject the *Vedas*. A misinterpretation of the *Vedas* by influential *brahmanas*/priests instigated the unprecedented turn to meat eating. So as a temporary measure, Lord Buddha taught everyone to reject the *Vedas* and follow the Buddhist path of non-violence, otherwise known as in Sanskrit as *ahmisa*. But little did Lord Buddha's followers know that He was non-different from the Lord who spoke the original *Vedas*....) And so it happened that shortly after Sankaracharya re-established the *Vedas* in India, Buddhism emerged in the surrounding Asiatic countries, including China. But Buddhism in India goes back even further than 3,500 years. According to the ancient writings of a great Indian Vaishnava poet, Jayadeva Gosvami, Lord Buddha is glorified as one of the *dashavatara*, ten incarnations of God, who appeared in a previous age dating back much further than 5,000 years. This point is also documented in the Vedic scripture *Bhagavata-purana*, otherwise known as *Srimad-Bhagavatam*. But over the last 2,500 years, owing to China's cultural intercourse with India, various forms of Buddhism are found in China today.

2. Martial Arts originated in India but later became prominent in China. The Indian origin of Martial Arts is verified by the fact that some of Kung Fu's fighting position terminologies – still used by some masters today – are original 5,000-year-old Sanskrit names.

3. The *Kama-sutra* is a Vedic writing said to have been compiled around 300 AC by the Indian sage Vatsayana. In the Chinese Taoist tradition there are sexual practices that closely resemble the erotic pleasure rituals portrayed in the *Kama-sutra*. Going back even further, some of India's ancient buildings portray sculptures depicting the various erotic positionings found in the *Kama-sutra*, confirming the Indian origin.

4. India's 5,000-year-old *Ayurveda* medicine cures diseases by treating the body's life-force centre known as *prana*, and the more recent Chinese medicine similarly corrects health problems by treating the 'chi', the body's life-force centre.

5. Corresponding to both these medical principles, the objective of the 5,000-year-old science of *Vastu* is to create a harmonious *prana*, or

VASTU - The Origin of Feng Shui

living space; while the more recent chinese Feng Shui also emphasises the importance of maintaining a healthy 'chi' in the home.

6. In *Vastu* there is the chanting of the ancient Vedic mantra: *om mahabhagavataya vastupurushaya svaha* for rectifying household spatial disharmony; and in Feng Shui, one of the ways to correct a disturbed chi in the house is to regularly chant nine times the mantra: *Om Ma Knee Pad Me Olm*. Reciting a mantra preceded by the syllable 'om', which invokes transcendence, comes from nowhere else but the *Vedas*.

The more we study both cultures the more we find that various aspects of Chinese culture originated from India's Vedic culture. Shortly after the Buddhists from India went to china, the Chinese Taoist tradition integrated the science of *Vastu* into their culture, adding and subtracting a few things here and there, until *Vastu* in that part of the world became known as Feng Shui (pronounced as *fong shuway*).

The different cultural and climatic conditions in China are the most likely explanations for the differences between *Vastu* and Feng Shui. For instance, the Chinese conclude that the north is generally an inauspicious direction because China had long received constant Mongol military threats from the north and always had cold northern winds. Whereas in *Vastu*, the North is always considered an auspicious direction, and this book explains why.

In Feng Shui, the five elements are earth, water, fire, metal, and wood and are said to represent the dynamic processes of transition. But in *Vastu*, the five elements are ether, air, fire, water, and earth whose influences are combined with Nature's wider range of physical laws and cosmic powers. The direct translation of Feng Shui is 'Wind and Water', the two elements of Nature that are said to shape our very existence. In ancient times both China and Greece divided Nature into five elements, but a complete analysis of their divisions would involve far too much detail to include in this book.

Vastu and Feng Shui are similar; but like a big and small dictionary, the overall difference lies mainly in the completeness. *Vastu*'s examination, for example, extends far beyond the energetic levels in and around your home. The great science of *Vastu* penetrates four levels: physical, energetic, karmic, and spiritual, involving all of Nature's auspicious and inauspicious energies emanating from the five great elements, the influential planets in Earth's sphere, and the powerful influences of the demigods and personalities controlling the eight directions of our universe.

In Chinese and Indian medicines we find similar parallels. The chi, life-force, in Chinese medicine is understood to flow between different bodily centres, which are assigned to certain bodily, mental, and psychological functions. In *Ayurveda*, those life-force centres are called chakras, and when they are not supplied with the 'right' energies a person becomes proportionately dysfunctional. But when all the life-force centres are properly supplied and working in harmony, one experiences good health, wisdom, and happiness.

In both *Vastu* and Feng Shui the same medicinal principles that are applied

Origin of Feng Shui

to the life-force of your body are also applied to the house, because your house is treated as the body of your body. In *Vastu*, for example, if your home is blocked to the auspicious influences flowing from the north, northeast, and east, and if your home is also open to the naturally inauspicious influences emanating from the south, southwest, and west, you accordingly encounter energetic blocks and negative energies that cause depression, loss of energy, disease, and many other adverse physiological and psychological effects. Just like a human body, every house 'breathes' through its front entrance a certain quality of 'life-force' or 'living space' that subsequently occupies, energises, and creates rooms of good, bad, or mixed energetic living qualities.

Books on *Vastu* and Feng Shui are currently on the increase because a large growing number of people understandably want to improve the quality of the 'living space' within their homes. Comparatively, the ancient Indian science of *Vastu*, which is the origin of Feng Shui, has remained far less known to the Western world. If you are already familiar with the principles of *Vastu* and Feng Shui, you'll certainly discover many more refinements in this book. With additional living insights and corrective tools, you'll access more of Nature's auspicious energies – enjoying a heavenly ambience and finer order with Nature – right in your own office and home, the places where we spend most of our lives.

Just as in Ayurveda the life energy is concentrated in different qualitative chakras in the body, in Vastu the flow of the prana or chi in a house creates rooms of various qualities.

Main Influences in Vastu

Five Great Elements

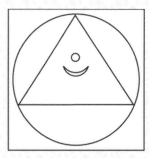

The purpose of the science of *Vastu* is to help you choose the right plot of land and correctly position your house so that you can keep bad influences out and enjoy all Nature's auspicious influences. The multifarious influences of the elements ether, air, fire, water, and earth; the Sun's heat and light; the climatic rain, wind, and temperature; the magnetic field of the earth; specific influential planets in the eight directions; and the powerful influence of the controlling demigods and personalities in the eight directions, all these gross and subtle energies are very carefully examined and accordingly balanced in *Vastu*.

The elements fire, water, and earth are present in our material bodies as well as the surrounding gross material Nature. The elements air and ether are found in higher dimensional or more subtle physical processes, as confirmed by modern natural sciences. The onus lies with an architect to avoid a clashing of Nature's five elements. This is achieved by simultaneously thinking, perceiving, and experiencing in harmony with Nature. Vedic architecture is a holistic, meditative, creative art of designing and building in harmony with all Nature's influences. Linear means of expression such as speech and script are insufficient to grasp the deepest intricacies of these complex interrelations. Humankind and Nature have always been mutually bound and dependent. Just as *Ayurveda* cures diseases by re-establishing the balance of the body's elements, one aspect of designing and building with *Vastu* is first understanding then balancing – in the living space of your buildings – the combined influence and order of Nature's five elements.

The Asana Mandala, a diagram of the combined five material elements.

Ether

The ether element refers to both the space in which your plot is located and the open living spaces inside your home. In *Vastu*, space, or the ether element, is not regarded as a vacuum but as an element with a complex inner structure that influences everything inside it. Ether can be manipulated not only by crafting light and spatial areas but also by creating various sounds because sound is the inner quality of ether. All kinds of sound vibrations inside your home, or even outside background noises, influence 'your' ether element and consequently the quality of the space in your living and working areas.

The mind, or the concept of a project, relates to both the ethereal area and to acoustics, including sound vibrations and even areas of silence. How all the subtle energies in and around your home communicate together is an essential factor in *Vastu* architecture. All that subtle phenomena – together with design and verbal expressions – is assigned to the ether element. In *Vastu*, the ether element is very important because of the distinctive influences of the eight directions upon the ether element in your home. Therefore, as will be explained herein, 'open spaces' both in your house and on your plot must be carefully treated and positioned.

The five elements are assigned to the secondary directions:

Earth - southwest
Water - northeast
Fire - southeast
Air - northwest
Ether - the centre

*A symbol of the element **ETHER**, which is best represented by space, vacuum, subtle forms, and sounds.*

Main Influences in Vastu

Air

The air element is perceived by the sense of touch. Air serves as the most important basis of life since our breathing and well-being are totally dependent upon the quality of air we breathe. By breathing we directly influence or experience the dynamics of the air element. In yoga, the process of controlling the breath is called *pranayama*. When executed properly *pranayama* improves your health, helps you gain control of your mind, and – as with the greatest yogis in days of old – can even give you the mystic ability to control the other elements.

The air element is related to architectural factors such as climatic conditions, building ecology, and various surface qualities that emulate the characteristics of touch and function. Air represents the principle of movement and refers to the gaseous aggregate. Although a building is primarily perceived as a static object, it is actually constantly moving because the walls of a building are constantly connected to the moving air element and flowing life-force.

The life-force of a house in Feng Shui is known as 'chi', and in *Vastu* it is called 'prana'. *Prana* means 'life-air' and represents the subtle air element. Feng Shui places great emphasis on not disturbing the harmonious flow of the life-air in your home, and the same applies in *Vastu*. According to the science of geomantics (geomechanics), the air of different geographical places contains good and bad qualities of life-force. Therefore good air quality and auspiciously positioned life-force points must be seriously taken into account when evaluating a plot for your office or home.

*A symbol of the element **AIR**, which is represented by movement, life energy, prana or chi, quantum processes, and touch.*

Fire

The influence of the fire element is most important because we have the ability to control fire and use it for many valuable purposes. In today's technologically driven society, fire is humankind's most manipulated element. Worldwide use of the fire element for vehicles and industry is disrupting the natural balance of the elements on the entire Earth. In fact, the excess use of the fire element has become so great that we are now faced with a dangerous overheating of the atmosphere, or global warming. The same principles of imbalance apply to your house. According to your house's positioning, you may have too much or too little exposure to the fire element's influence which lies to the southeast of your premises. *Vastu* explains herein how to achieve the right balance of the fire element.

Fire represents the energy of light and heat and is closely connected to the subtle principle of form. The fire element has its origin in the Sun and we perceive the various forms and colours of the fire element with our eyes and sense of touch. In *Vastu*, the form of a plot and the form of a building are subject to rigid specifications because the movement of the Sun in regard to the house and the plot is of crucial importance. Correctly positioning your heating outlets and kitchen, as explained herein, are also important because auspicious usage of the fire element in your office or home enhances wealth and prosperity and many other aspects of your life.

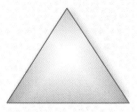

*A symbol of the element **FIRE**, which is represented by heat, light, electricity, form, and colour.*

Five Great Elements

Water

Water represents the flowing aspect of time and expresses itself most prominently in aesthetics. Nature's water cycles are intervened by Architecture to create new subsystem cycles such as water and sewerage systems. The water element is perceived as taste and is opposed to fire. The water cycles of both Nature and your home are circulated by means of the fire element. The dynamic interaction of water and fire in the Sun's absorbing water and showering rain is indispensable for human life. But the more we disturb this finely tuned system with various pollutants the more the system of life and the environment of our planet becomes dysfunctional. The same finely tuned system applies wherever there is the use of water and fire in buildings. And if your water distribution and fire energies are correctly positioned, Nature endows your surroundings with harmony and success.

Water is the basis of life but it is also an element that must be kept at a safe distance. The rainfall in your area; the flood potential from nearby rivers, streams, and springs; underground water currents and the ground-water level; and the arrangement of your drinking water must all be examined very closely. As explained herein, the correct positioning of water wells, large water reservoirs like a swimming pool, or water fountain influences the quality of your life and the success of your work.

*A symbol of the element **WATER**, which is represented by vibration, expansion, feelings, and taste.*

Earth

The earth element forms the basis of life since we live in an earthen environment and have earthly bodies in a combined solid state. The earth element is represented by the condition of the soil, flora, and fauna in all our surrounding landscapes. These earthly items are like a sculptor's tools for us to create, change, and design Nature around us. The earth element is connected to all areas of smell and is assigned to the generative systems, the design of the landscape, and the plant world. The sense qualities of all other elements are contained in the earth element for it is endowed with sound, touch, form, smell, and taste. The significant influences of subtle earth energies and magnetic fields are assigned to the earth element. As will be explained, obtaining the right shape, slope, and quality of the earth element for your plot of land is just as important as selecting the right building materials.

The *Ayurveda* explains how the positive energies of the five elements can be accessed:

Ether *watching the sky and stars is to access the ether element that helps maintain a balanced psychological disposition*

Air inhaling the breath of the plants provides the best breathing air which is vital for good health

Fire bathing in the morning sunshine is to access the fire element and obtain the most natural form of Vitamin D which helps to maintain strong teeth and bones

*A symbol of the element **EARTH**, which is represented by gravity, consolidation, magnetism, structure, mass, electric charge, and smell.*

Influential Planets in Earth's Sphere

Earth, water, fire, air, ether, mind, intelligence, and false ego - all together these eight elements comprise My separated material energies. (Bhagavad-gita As It Is, Ch. 4.4)

Water *drinking only the purest water is a sure way to good health because the human body is largely made up of water*

Earth *walking with bare feet on the earth enables absorption of the auspicious energies of the earth element.*

Just as your body requires a certain balanced mix of the five elements, your house – which is the body of your body – also requires the correct exposure to the five elements to obtain a healthy balanced living space.

Influential Planets in Earth's Sphere

Knowing the specific influences of certain planets upon the eight directional areas of your home and office, and then positioning different room functions accordingly, greatly enhances the harmony of the living space in your entire home (see diagram on page 29). The following are some basic guidelines:

The Sun

The Sun planet's auspicious influences are strongest in the east of your home. Rooms in the east or northeast are good for prayer, worship, and meditation. Respecting the Sun planet in this way is auspicious since the *Vedas* state that by worshipping the Sun one becomes blessed with good health. Looking at your main entrance from the inside, the right side window and room are ruled by the male energy of the Sun and is therefore good for male occupancy (but not detrimental to females).

The Moon

The moon planet's influence is strongest in the northwest. If you have good Vastu in the northwest, your fame and honour are increased, and your relationships are benefited. Viewing your main entrance from the inside, the left side window and room are ruled by the female energy of the Moon and is subsequently good for female occupancy (but not detrimental for males). The moon also rules the bathroom, water storage, cow shed, and journeys.

Mars

Mars lies to the south of your home. Although Mars has some very inauspicious influences, Mars can give tremendous strength and wealth, depending upon your personal horoscope. Wealth from Mars comes to those with a well placed southeast kitchen as well as a correctly positioned chimney and fireplace/s. Vastu defects in the south invite various losses and problems, but good Vastu in the south inspires religiosity, justice, strong discipline, and power.

Main Influences in Vastu

Mercury

Mercury lies to the north of your home. With good Vastu in the north, Mercury fosters study, business, communication, and good character. Mercury also rules areas that function as the entrance hall, green areas, a veranda, and office.

Jupiter

Jupiter lies to the northeast of your home. With good Vastu in the northeast, Jupiter strengthens character, awards respect, influences the room containing one's most valuable possessions, favours a children's bedroom in the northeast, and nurtures spiritual development.

Venus

Venus lies to the southeast of your home. With good Vastu in the southeast, Venus enhances fine speech and benefits sofas, living rooms, dining rooms, bedrooms, and women with auspiciousness.

Saturn

Saturn lies to the west of your home. Through a main entrance in the west, Saturn influences inauspicious circumstances such as divorce, depression, uncontrollable sexuality, and general delays. On the positive side, if you have good Vastu in the west, i.e. the west is more closed than open, Saturn engenders auspicious qualities such as popularity, scholarship, happiness, and good eating. In a building with good Vastu, Saturn bestows auspiciousness on the store rooms, eating and hunger, the garbage area, and the energy flow between front and back entrances.

Rahu and Ketu

Although the planets Rahu and Ketu are not known in Western astrology, they play an important role in Vedic astrology. Ketu's auspicious influence comes to your office or home from the northeast and Rahu's inauspicious influence from the southwest. Thus good Vastu in the northeast is to have dipped and open land, and good Vastu in the southwest is to have those inside and outside areas raised and blocked. Facing your front entrance from outside, Rahu rules the right side and Ketu governs the left. With good Vastu their combined influence provides a protective influence all around your home. Rahu also rules the entire main entrance, as well as big dark rooms and big doors. Ketu rules the exit, bathrooms, and cracked or broken walls. A more detailed description of this subject, which is beyond the scope of this book, will be addressed in a future Vasati edition. For an overview of the influential planets in the eight directions see the diagram on page 29.

The Vedas combine the importance of material and spiritual knowledge. The science of Vastu, Vedic architecture, is therefore both a material and spiritual science with immense spiritual and material benefits.

Controllers of the Eight Directions

The demigods assigned to each of the planets in Earth's sphere exert their influence upon us by the movements of their planets. The eight directional areas in your office or home are influenced by the controlling demigods as follows:

Indra in the <u>EAST</u>

*The **EAST** is considered to be the best of all directions. When sleeping, eating, cooking, or praying one should be facing east.*

The demigod Indra is the embodiment of power and strength, and the ruler of many other demigods. The Sun rises in the east and therefore the east is the most prominent direction. Good Vastu in the east increases health, wealth, and prosperity. The eastern part of your plot should not be completely covered by the house, otherwise the paternal relationship becomes adversely affected. The east is divided into nine aspects among which the Sun, fire, truth, victory, Shiva, and Heaven are the most important.

Varuna in the <u>WEST</u>

*Bedrooms for children and male inhabitants should be located in the **WEST**, representing peace and sunset.*

The demigod Varuna is the controller of all the oceans, representing silence and pride. Good Vastu in the west bestows glory, fame, learning, and prosperity. The west has nine aspects among which disease, sin, a cobra, a demon, a gatekeeper, and the ancestors are the most prominent.

Kuvera in the <u>NORTH</u>

*One should avoid sleeping in the north of the house, and sleeping with one's head toward the **NORTH**.*

The demigod Kuvera is the treasurer of the demigods, embodying wealth and prosperity. Good Vastu in the north attracts wealth. But if there is no space in the north, not only are finances adversely affected but the females and motherly relationships suffer because the north represents the maternal energy. Therefore the north of your plot should not be completely covered by your house, and the shape of your land should be according to the good Vastu guidelines on pages 33-35. Diti and Aditi (the mothers of the demigods and demons respectively), the snake, and the Moon are assigned to the north.

Yamaraja in the <u>SOUTH</u>

*The **SOUTH** is ideal for a bedroom, and a good direction to have your head pointing during sleep. A main entrance in the south should be avoided.*

The demigod Yamaraja is the Lord of death and religious principles (dharma). This direction is not beneficial for auspicious activities and should not be the location of your front entrance. Good Vastu in the south, i.e. blocking the south's negative influences, enhances general prosperity.

Agni in the <u>SOUTHEAST</u>

*All arrangements with fire, heat, electricity, and the generation of energy should be placed in the **SOUTH-EAST** of the house and each room.*

The demigod Agni is the Lord of fire. Good Vastu in this direction benefits one with a healthy, controllable sexuality for having healthy children with a good disposition. The southeast of your home is also the best position for the kitchen, and such positioning greatly enhances health and prosperity. The southeast is best for agnihotras, or Vedic fire ceremonies.

Main Influences in Vastu

Nairutva and Putana in the <u>SOUTHWEST</u>

Two demoniac personalities rule the southwest. One is the powerful female demon, Putana, and the other is the king of the demons, Nairutva. They are equal to demigods in power and status, but are demoniac by nature. The southwest therefore should not be used for any auspicious purposes. The southwest represents the character and behaviour of a person and is connected to the length of one's life. It is best to fill up this direction with heavy immovable things. Under no circumstances should there be any water storage, toilets, or bathrooms in the southwest. Vastu defects in this direction negatively influence one's moral attitude and behaviour. However, good Vastu in the southwest, to have this direction blocked as much as possible, strengthens one's power and influence in all walks of life.

*The **SOUTHWEST** should be closed as much as possible and have maximum weight.*

Vayu in the <u>NORTHWEST</u>

The demigod Vayu is the lord of the wind. The circulation of air or wind is essential for the vitality and health of all living entities. Subsequently you should not have any tall buildings or trees in your northwest. Good Vastu in this direction greatly enhances your personal relationships and general hospitality, a quality most important for social harmony. The northwest therefore is the most auspicious area in your home for entertaining guests.

The **NORTHWEST** is ideal for anything moveable such as cars, bicycles, guests, animals, and business transactions. This direction influences change, the element of lightness, and relationships.

Ishan in the <u>NORTHEAST</u>

God himself, otherwise known in Vedic culture as Ishan, or Lord Vishnu, rules the northeast. He is the controller of all other controllers. This direction on your plot should never be covered with any unnecessary objects but left open and clear. However, underground water storage or wells in the northeast yield auspiciousness. Either inside or outside your house, there should not be any toilets in the northeast. The northeast represents the male family succession and greatly assists those pursuing spiritual development.

*The **NORTHEAST** is the direction of purity and the divine. The northeast of your plot and house should always be clean, light, and tidy. A toilets should never be in the northeast.*

The eight directions are found in illustrations from all civilisations:

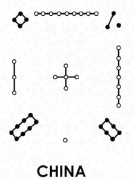

CHINA

INDIA

AFRICA

Main Influences in Vastu

Morning Sunshine

It is all too easy to overlook the importance of having sufficient sunshine in our lives. *Vastu* therefore recommends positioning your home to get maximum benefit. The Sun is the cosmic representation of the element fire. A prime example of how the individual elements interact is clearly visible in the opposing elements fire and water. For instance, water absorbs photons from sunshine and reflects or directly transmits them to human beings. Modern biophysics confirm that photons stored in water constitute a vital part of the human organism. Therefore the Sun's rays not only supply human beings with energy and heat but provide information, order, and food for the body. When the Sun's rays touch your skin or eyes, nutritious photons and the most natural form of Vitamin D are absorbed into your body and stored by the cell cores of the organism. There are only a few foods that contain significant amounts of vitamin D, and the most commonly consumed vitamin D containing foods are fortified dairy products.

The big problem with dietary intake of vitamin D is that it is a fat-soluble vitamin which lives in fat droplets. Sports people and those dieting from fat intake subsequently restrict themselves from vitamin D. Taking vitamin D supplements is not a good idea because vitamin D is the most potentially toxic of all vitamins. However, vitamin D is readily available in Nature's morning sunshine.

Morning sunshine contains an ultraviolet light which changes a form of cholesterol in your skin to vitamin D. The vitamin D is then transported to the parts of the body that need it. The amount of sun exposure needed to produce vitamin D depends on several factors: skin colour, age, and climate. People with dark skin, older people, and people in northern climates require more time in the sun than others. Most people can manufacture enough vitamin D in the summer to last them through the winter and there's little danger of an overdose on sunlight vitamin D because the body limits the amount formed. Why is vitamin D important? It facilitates the absorption of calcium, regulates calcium and phosphorus metabolism in the body, and helps build strong bones and teeth.

In Biophysics, the term bio-photons has been coined in order to underline the special meaning of the Sun's light for humans. Water has the ability of storing photons coming from the Sun and reflecting or directly transmitting them to human beings. This phenomena is taken into account in *Vastu*, even though to our knowledge the ancient sages of India did not have any observation photon multipliers. Modern science is now slowly verifying age old concepts that were previously thought to be myths, particularly on how the elements interact.

The Sun, which is the source of all light and heat, generally rises in the east and sets in the west. But depending upon what part of the world you are in, the position of the sunrise and sunset fluctuates by varying degrees in the course of a year. In some countries, the availability of any sunshine at all is also a factor, and in those places even the afternoon Sun is better than nothing. We receive the auspicious morning sunshine from either the east, northeast, or southeast and are thus benefited with positive influences for the body, house, and land. Therefore you should avoid building anything on those areas of your plot that give entrance to the morning sunshine. And strictly avoid having a toilet in the northeast of your plot because the beneficial effects of the Sun's rays are reversed by the sewage water.

The light of the Sun from the southeast onto the plot has a different quality and therefore the southeast should not be used to store water. The difference is that southeast sunlight contains infrared rays that have a negative influence on human organisms. The rising Sun gives vitality and health to your body whereas the afternoon sunshine has the opposite effect. Of course in countries where there is very little Sun the afternoon rays, which are not too strong anyway, inject an otherwise dull area with an uplifting light. In climates where there is plenty or even too much sunshine, it is best to block the afternoon sunrays with tall trees or large constructions. Since water reservoirs store the positive or negative energy of sunshine and light, under no circumstances should there be any water reservoirs in the southwest from which inauspicious energies emanate. For the same reason the walls surrounding the premises should be lower in the northeast than in the southwest. The number of windows in the southwest should be reduced to a minimum.

Vastu assigns a special meaning to the various parts of sunlight, i.e. the components of the spectrum. There are seven rays of the Sun to which *Vastu* assigns universal principles represented by cosmic entities. Those seven rays consist of light in seven colours which have a positive or negative effect according to the time of day and the direction from which they emanate. The day is divided into seven sections, each with its specific colour.

The UV light of the Sun reduces blood pressure, increases the performance of the heart, improves the ECG and blood values of patients suffering from arteriosclerosis. UV light also reduces cholesterol values and is effective against psoriasis and activates important skin hormones.

Sun's manifold colours

Violet is 3.00 pm to 4.30 pm

The early morning is known as brahma-muhurta to which the demigod Indra, the embodiment of power, is assigned. This period is defined as one and a half hours before sunrise. Indra destroys darkness and leads us to the light of truth. This section of the day is the best for meditation and worship of God. Even in India today, many people still rise during the *brahma-muhurta* to perform spiritual activities and practice yoga in order to begin the day strengthened and well prepared. The sunrays' colour during this period is violet.

Indigo is 4.30 pm to 6 pm

In the second period, the birds begin chirping and singing, and other animals begin their day. The whole of Nature becomes filled with new life, energy, and strength. The ruler of this time period is Kashyapa. *Ayurveda* states that it is detrimental to one's health if one rises later than this period. The colour of the sunrays during this period is indigo.

Blue is 6.00 pm to 9.00 pm

In the third period the sunrays are spread everywhere and people begin to perform their daily tasks. The colour of the sunrays during this period is blue.

The Sun's ultra-violet light of the Sun is a nutrient to the body just like vitamins or minerals. Most people can manufacture enough vitamin D in summer to last them through the winter and there's little danger of ODing on sunlight vitamin D because the body limits the amount formed.

Each individual quality of the eight directions is related to the movements of the Sun which, depending upon the respective time, shines from a different direction and in a different colour. At the same time the direction of Earth's magnetic field and the effect of the Moon's gravitation also have a significant influence.

During your life there are innumerable influences, among which your house and immediate environment are most significant. More important than your house being a comfortable shelter from extreme weather conditions is harmonising your living and working spaces with all Nature's multifarious influences.

Green is 9.00 am to 12.00 a.m

In the fourth period the speed of everyone's activities is raised. This phase is under the rule of the Sun, which reaches its peak at 12.00 midday. The colour of the sunrays during this period is green.

Yellow is 12.00 am to 3.00 pm

In the fifth period of the day the afternoon commences and the sunrays turn toward the west. These rays are not as beneficial as the morning sun. Truth is the ruler of this period. The sunrays' colour during this period is yellow.

Orange is 3.00 pm to 6.00 pm

In the sixth period of the day the afternoon Sun has a negative effect on humankind. The colour of the sunrays during this period is orange.

Red is 6.00 pm to 7.30 pm

In the seventh period of the day the light of the Sun quickly diminishes and darkness spreads, and the day's activities come to an end. The colour of the sunrays during this period is red.

The colours of the seven rays of the Sun are also assigned to the directions, which are also closely connected to the course of the Sun. The ultra-violet segment of the sunlight corresponds to the northeast direction, which is considered to be the purest. The southeast, connected with the fire element, is related to the infrared segment of the Sun spectrum. The allocation of the other rays of the Sun to individual periods of the day, demigods, and directions indicates the deep physical connection which also depends upon the composition and structure of the atmosphere of the earth. A detailed examination of the Vedic scriptures in this regard would provide important impulses for modern physical science.

Earth's magnetic field (magnetosphere)

All magnetic objects produce invisible lines of force that extend between the poles of an object. An easy way to visualise this is to spread iron filings on a sheet of paper and place a bar magnet under the paper. The iron filings will arrange themselves around the magnet and along the magnetic field lines.

In the simplest terms, Earth can be thought of as a dipole (2-pole) magnet. Magnetic field lines radiate between Earth's north and south magnetic poles just as they do between the poles of a bar magnet. Charged particles become trapped on these field lines (as the iron filings are trapped), forming the magnetosphere.

Earth's magnetic field lines are not as symmetrical as those of the bar magnet. The impact of the solar wind causes the lines facing sunward to compress, while the field lines facing away from the Sun stream back to form Earth's magneto tail. The magnetosphere extends into the vacuum of space from approximately 80 to 60,000 kilometres (50 to 37,280 miles) on the side toward the Sun, and trails out more than 300,000 kilometres (186,500 miles) away from the Sun.

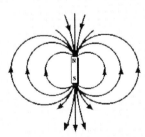

The energy flow of a bar magnet reflects Earth's energy flow.

Earth's Magnetic Field

Both the Earth planet and your body have related magnetic properties. The magnetic field of Earth goes from north to south, and the magnetic north and south of your body goes from your head to your feet. If you sleep with your head pointing north, Earth's north pole and your north pole repel each other, resulting in poor blood circulation, an altered heartbeat, and a restless sleep. The opposite is achieved by sleeping with your head pointing south, because opposite poles attracting each other promote a healthy and peaceful sleep.

The gravity of the Moon, which causes the swelling of tides, also has an influence on your body. With the waxing and waning of the moon your body fluids accordingly rise and fall. Women are more affected by this than men, therefore the southeast influences women more than men. In the science of *Vastu*, each of the eight directions has specific qualities that influence everything moving and non-moving in its direction of influence. Those various influences of the eight directions are best perceived in a square or rectangle shape with eight subsections, as shown in the following diagrams.

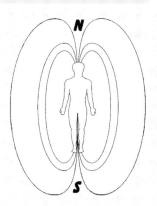

The human magnetic energy flow.

This diagram summarises the predominant metaphysical and astrological qualities of the eight directions. In each direction there is one or more *controlling demigod*, ruling planet, predominating element, and affected bodily organ.

Vayu Moon **air** stomach/spleen/anus	*Kuvera* Mercury **water/air** thymus/throat	*Ishan* Jupiter/Ketu **water/ether** brain/head
Varuna Saturn **earth/air/water** kidneys/abdomen	(compass diagram: N, NW, NE, W, E, SW, SE, S)	*Indra* Sun **ether/fire** heart
Nairutva Rahu **earth** feet/bones	*Yamaraja* Mars **earth/fire** kidneys/abdomen	*Agni* Venus **fire** liver

Main Influences in Vastu

Metaphysical principles of a cosmic Nature act upon the directions which in *Vastu* have always been related to the characteristics of various demigods. These demigods represent the complementary aspect of truth, or God, who unifies all qualities in Himself and balances all dualities. *Vastu* concludes that if one knows and practices the principles concerning the qualities of the eight directions then one has mastered the science of ideal building and living space.

With good all round Vastu in a house or office, various good qualities are invoked and certain persons are most influenced

loving relationships purposeful movement productive exchanges mother and 1st son	*auspicious birth* capital assets positive cash flow women & daughters	*spirituality* knowledge intellectual ability father & sons
peacefulness conclusive endings good education sons		*auspicious beginning* power health sons
weight influence expansion father, mother, 1st son	*wealth* power discipline women & daughters	*dynamic energy levels* powerful acceleration controllable sexuality women, children, 2nd son

Mother Nature's general positive influences on people in buildings with good Vastu

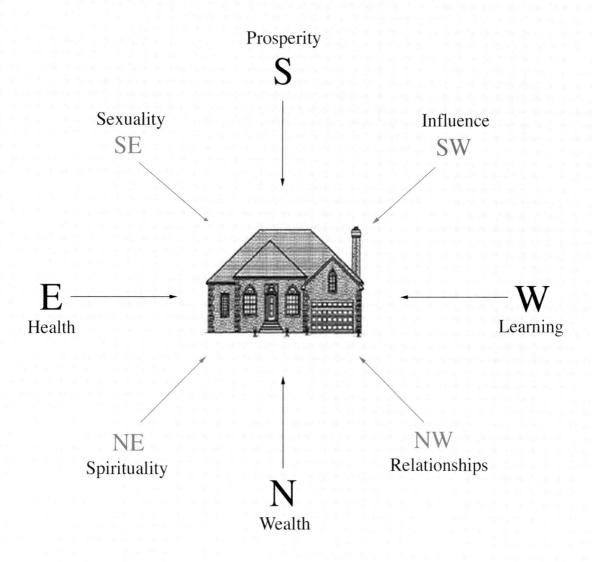

Prosperity
S

Sexuality
SE

Influence
SW

E
Health

W
Learning

NE
Spirituality

NW
Relationships

N
Wealth

Check Your Land Attributes for Good Vastu

If you have the good fortune of being able to choose your own plot of land and build your own house, this section will give you valuable guidance. If you don't have that option (and that applies to most of us) you'll still benefit from carefully reading this section because you'll need to ascertain what defects your house and land have and then correct them as recommended in the 'How to Easily Remove up to 98% of Defects' section on page 81.

What follows are ten basic check points to consider when observing the Vastu qualities of an existing or prospective plot of land:

Land slope

The slope of your land significantly influences the quality of your household. In general the south and west should be higher so that your land slopes towards an open north and east. This ideal land slope absorbs Nature's auspiciousness from the north and east and evades the inauspicious influences from the south and west. Such a slope also causes rainwater to flow auspiciously from west to north and south to east.

The ground level beneath a building should be higher in the south, southwest, and west in comparison to the north, northeast, and east. It is most auspicious if the northeast is the deepest point. If the ground contradicts these confines, try to move the earth so that the proportions give you an auspicious slope. The expenses incurred will be 'naturally' recuperated many times over.

Never allow any out-buildings in the northwest, northeast, or southeast quadrants to directly touch the compound wall or to be connected to the house. The ground level of northeast out-buildings or water compounds must be lower than the floor of the main building.

Land shape

The most auspicious length and width ratio for a plot of land is a 1:1 square. Subsequent rectangular ratios from 1:1 on up to 1:2 are also auspicious. But the more the proportions exceed the ratio 1:2 the less conducive the plot becomes for containing, balancing, and utilising Nature's multifarious influences. If the plot's ratio must exceed the ideal 1:1 square and form a rectangle, a longer north to south side is best.

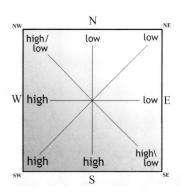

The ideal plot is square or rectangular and is elevated in the south and west. Mountains in the west and south are ideal, and so is a river or stream in the north or east. The soil should have a good aroma and be fertile.

If the front entrance side of a plot is longer than the back, the plot is better suited for business.

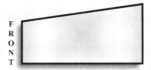

If the front entrance side of a plot is not as wide as the back, the plot is better suited as a residence.

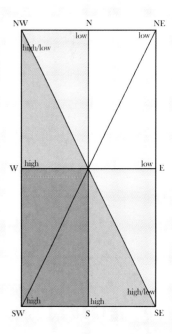

An ideal land slope on a rectangular plot

The plot corners should not point to the main directions but rather to the secondary directions. A rectangular plot with sides facing the main directions is also good. Circular or triangular plots are not harmonious and prevent stability. If the plot must be round then only a round building should be erected. A building on a round plot should never be pentagonal, hexagonal, or completely irregular. If an irregularly shaped plot cannot be avoided, the inauspiciousness can be avoided by selecting a square or rectangular part of the plot and partitioning that portion of land with an interior wall or suitable fence. In this way Nature's energies can be more easily concentrated and harmonised.

An octagonal shaped plot or house is very auspicious.

A pentagonal form should be turned into a rectangular form by division or supplementation.

If a round plot can't be avoided, then construct only a round building.

This plot shape exceeds 1:2 and should be accordingly subdivided.

This shape is not good. The angles should be balanced so that only the northeast is expanded.

A triangle shaped plot obstructs progress and invites problems with the government.

Round and irregular round forms should be avoided.

This irregular shape can be corrected as indicated.

This irregular shape can be partitioned off to create an auspicious rectangle shape.

Check Your Land Attributes for Good Vastu

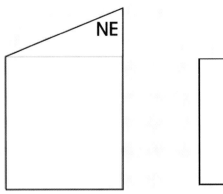 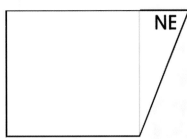

Expansions to the northeast are auspicious

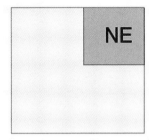

An L-shaped plot with the northeast missing is inauspicious.

Soil condition

It is best if the soil is light, yellow, or red. If the soil takes on a black colour under 3.6m, the inhabitants will have to work hard without decisive improvement. Before starting construction, any objects on the land such as iron, steel, ripped clothes, bones, cotton, ant hills, termites, coal, and other such things must be removed. This will prevent any inauspicious influences from entering through the soil.

Land history

Vastu scriptures strongly recommend not to buy a plot of land or house in which the previous owner committed suicide, was bankrupted, crazy, diseased, or experienced any other such misfortune. Such histories cling to land and buildings with lingering effects that inevitably rub off on subsequent occupants to one degree or another.

Adjacent buildings

The position of a plot in relation to its neighbouring houses should be given very careful consideration. If there is a small plot between two big plots it should not be purchased. The same applies to small buildings between two big buildings. Such a purchaser will gradually lose wealth. Buildings blocking the northeast of your plot will cause you mental restlessness. Rain water from neighbouring plots should not flow into your plot, particularly from the north or east.

The most important factor when selecting the plot is its relative position to the magnetic meridian which should be parallel to the axis of the plot. A tolerance of 10° is acceptable. When the four corners of a plot or building point to the four main directions, the positive effects of *Vastu* are reduced. However, that does not mean one should not buy such a plot because it may be possible to re-shape the land and thereafter auspiciously position a house or office.

It is most auspicious to have a cow or calf graze on a plot before beginning construction. Properly maintained cows look for places of positive energy and attract good energies.

Surrounding Streets

Streets on all four sides

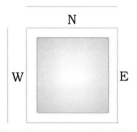

The position of the streets around a plot also play an important role. A building with streets on all four sides is considered very auspicious. Such a location indicates health, wealth, prosperity, and a balanced mind. If such a house/office is in the northeast of a village, there will be an enormous increase in wealth, business, and knowledge. The southeast of a town or village offers the ideal position for hotels or any manufacturing plant that involves the fire element.

Streets on three sides

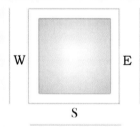

Streets in the east, west, and north of a plot are very good and foster wealth and prosperity. But one should make sure that the main gate to the plot is in the north, and there should be more open space available in the north and east than in the south and west.

Streets in the east, west, and south have very positive effects on business, and the main gate should be east.

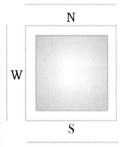

Streets in the south, west, and north are also good but the main entrance should be in the west, and the east should have more open space.

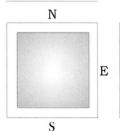

Streets in the east, south, and north of a plot are also very good if the main gate or entrance is in the east.

Check Your Land Attributes for Good Vastu

Streets on two sides

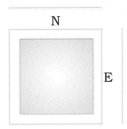

Streets in the north and east of a plot are very auspicious. A main entrance in the east with more space in the north is best. And a main entrance in the north with more space in the east is also very good.

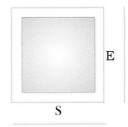

Streets in the east and south of a plot influence the inhabitants to spend excessively on entertainment. A south main entrance will make matters worse whereas an east entrance combined with more space in the east and north may help.

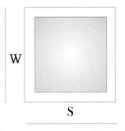

Streets in the south and west of a plot are not too bad if the main entrance is in the west. But a south entrance may incur heavy losses.

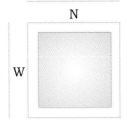

Streets in the north and west of a plot are good for money if the main entrance is in the north with more space in the north and east.

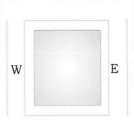

Streets in the west and east of a plot are good if the main entrance is in the east.

Streets in the north and south of a plot are also good if the main entrance is in the north.

A street on one side

A street on the north or east side is auspicious. If there is a street in the west, it fosters fame and honour. And a street in the south is mainly advantageous for businesses involving ladies' articles or entertainment products.

Streets leading directly to a plot

Streets which lead to the plot from the northeast (in the northern and eastern part), from the northwest (only in the western part) and from the southeast (only in the southern part) are considered as auspicious. On the other hand, streets are regarded as inauspicious if they lead from the north to the northwest of the plot or when they lead from the west or south to the southwest or from the east to the southeast. One should not acquire a plot situated at the end of a dead-end street that is in line with any of the main directions.

Surrounding area

Make sure there are no nuclear waste sites within a ten mile radius and air or noise polluting factories within a five mile radius. Keep your home or office away from an electric sub-station — at least 500 metres — because research indicates that prolonged exposure to such intense electro magnetic output is likely to effect one's health negatively. Avoid living too close to an airport since studies show that the constant noise of aeroplanes taking off can disrupt children's concentration on their education. Also avoid being too close to any waste site.

Rivers - canals

Rivers or canals that flow close to the plot in the north create auspiciousness, particularly if they flow from west to east. The same applies to rivers in the east if they flow from south to north. However, if there is a river in either the west or south the plot should be avoided.

Hills - mountains

Hills and mountains in the south, southwest, or west of the plot are good. But if they are located in the opposite directions they obstruct progress.

The land's orientation and your work

Every plot of land and house faces a particular direction. Such orientation is determined by the direction to which the plot slopes. A plot that is oriented towards the east will favour scholars, philosophers, priests, professors, and teachers. A plot that slopes to the north fosters people engaged in government administration and service. A plot directed toward the south supports those active in business, farming, and various economic ventures. And a plot oriented towards the west is ideal for people in the service and entertainment industries.

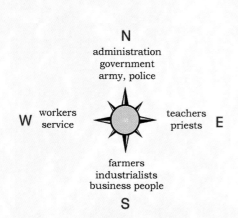

N
administration
government
army, police

W workers
service

teachers
priests E

farmers
industrialists
business people

S

Check Your Land Attributes for Good Vastu

A *bhumi-puja* ceremony for a new plot of land

If you have the good fortune to be able to buy an auspicious plot of land, Vastu recommends that you pay your respects to Mother Earth by worshipping the land before commencing construction. The ceremony for worshipping Mother Earth is called *bhumi-puja*. Thoroughly clean the entire plot of all unwanted things. The precise timing of the ceremony and commencement of construction should be calculated by an experienced astrologer familiar with the principles of Vastu. Having duly worshiped Earth, the digging of the soil should proceed clockwise and must not begin in the southwest. Where applicable, one should not dig a water well before constructing the building. Contact a Vasati consultant for advice on how best to have an auspicious *bhumi-puja* ceremony for your land.

The square is considered to be the perfect form because in it the polar opposites are brought into balance.

Check Your Outside Placements

Front gate/s - position

There are various auspicious positions for the gates to your plot. The best positions are obtained by dividing the wall into nine segments and then positioning the gate as follows: In the north the gate should be built in segment **5, 6, or 7**, in the east segment **3 or 4**, and in the west segment **5 or 6**. An entrance in the south is generally avoided but segment **4** is minimally beneficial for women if there is also another balancing entrance in either the north or east. It is better to have two entrances to your plot and house so that Nature's negative energies will not remain and cause disturbances.

Correctly positioned gates in the north and east give rise to wealth and fame. Correctly positioned gates in the west and east foster wealth and prosperity. Correctly positioned gates in the north and west enhance wealth and spirituality. A correctly positioned single gate either in the east or north also leads to wealth. A correctly positioned single gate in the west helps business blossom for a few years and then stagnate. Avoid a single plot entrance gate in the south because this will attract losses and difficulties.

Front gate - obstacles

The following problems are invoked from Nature if certain obstacles lie in front of your main gate:

1. *A tall tree obstructs children's progress.*
2. *A hole arouses anger and depression.*
3. *An open well invites mental problems.*
4. *The corner of another building leads to mental restlessness.*
5. *A waterfall induces financial losses.*
6. *Columns and poles negatively affect females.*
7. *Dilapidated houses, walls, or fences threaten wealth.*
8. *Stairs cause sadness.*

House position on land

Let's assume you have an ideal square plot, or a next best rectangular plot as described herein. The next step is to plan your house's exact position on the land. This is very important. *Vastu* divides your plot into four equal quadrants: the northwest, northeast, southeast, and the southwest. The main building should be erected in the southwest quadrant and not touch any boundary. Thus the eastern and northern sides of your plot will be open to the highly beneficial morning sunshine

The best positions for gates into a plot

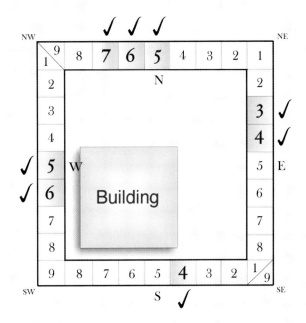

A plot's main entrance is best in the north or east. The west is less preferable, and in the south only the fourth segment is favourable. If other positions in the south can't be avoided, then at least one more entrance should be built in the north or east so that the negative energies from the south will flow through.

and the auspicious energies emanating from those directions. The northwest and northeast quadrants of your land should not have any big buildings.

Similar to the ideal plot size, the most auspicious length and width ratio for a house or office building is a 1:1 square. Subsequent rectangular ratios from 1:1 on up to 1:2 are also acceptable. But the more the proportions exceed the ratio 1:2 the less conducive the house becomes for containing, balancing, and utilising Nature's multifarious influences. If a building's ratio must exceed the ideal 1:1 square to form a rectangle, a longer north to south side is best.

Qualitative usage of the four quadrants

Vastu divides an ideal square or rectangular plot into four equal quadrants: the northwest, northeast, southeast, and the southwest. Each quadrant has a different quality and must therefore be used accordingly.

The southwest quadrant is assigned to the earth element and is the best place for the main building. Strictly avoid having any water storage, water pipes, or wet walls in this area. The rule is that the southwest corner should be heavy and closed while the other three quadrants should remain light and open. If the northwest, northeast, and southeast are closed with buildings, extensions, tall trees, and so on the inflow of positive energies will be blocked and negative energies will enter.

The northwest quadrant is assigned to the air element and this area is therefore best used for food storage, a garage, car parking, stable, and shed. An open northwest provides access for the wind and the air element. If this corner is closed it may have a negative influence on one's business transactions. Any outhouse buildings in this direction should not be too big and should have a distance of at least 60 - 90 cm from any wall.

The northeast quadrant is assigned to the water element and is therefore best suited for drinking water storage, a fountain, swimming pool, pond, and garden. The well or water tank should not be located directly in front of the plot entrance, they should be on either side of the entrance. A well should not be placed on the plot's northeast to southwest diagonal: the well should be located either to the left or right of that diagonal. Anything with water in the northeast is auspicious because the water absorbs and reflects the highly beneficial ultraviolet Sun rays. Drinking water which has been energised in that way supplies human body cells with bio-photons which are an important health giving sector of the light spectrum. The open space in the north and east is ideal for a garden, and the sitting benches there should be located in the west and south area with a view to the north and east.

The southeast quadrant is assigned to the fire element and is therefore best suited for out-buildings with technical or electrical systems that contain the fire element. Water and fire are not compatible and so there should be no water storage in the southeast. Nor should there be any electrical or fire equipment in

---

The southwest quadrant of the plot is best for the main building and heavy equipment. The northwest is suited for moveable things such as vehicles, animals, and grains. The northeast is best for water supply and garden. And the southeast is ideal for electrical or energy equipment that contains the fire element.

Stone gardens and sculptures should be placed in the southwest sector of the garden.

Garbage should never be stored in the northeast of your plot or building. The northeast must always be kept completely neat, clean, and tidy.

In the southwest of the house there should not be any water, moisture, or water installations.

the northeast. Southeast out-buildings must exceed 90 cm from a wall. The open space in the southeast enhances the fire element by connecting with the sunlight's infrared rays. When planning the open space around the house, make sure there is more space in the north and east than in the south and west. That open space allows the house to receive not only the beneficial morning sunshine but all the northern and eastern directions' auspicious influences.

Buildings with irregular forms

The shapes of residential or office buildings are best if they are mainly square or rectangular. L-shaped buildings are common but they are imbalanced because of the weight in the built-up area compared to the empty space. The following diagrams demonstrate the disadvantages of L-shaped buildings:

NW open

Residents of an L-shaped building that has an open northwest may experience turmoil in communications and relationships.

open NE

Residents of an L-shaped building that has an open northeast are minimally benefited with knowledge and general prosperity.

SW open

Residents of an L-shaped building that has an open southwest may endure various misfortunes from the southwest's negative energies.

open SE

Residents of an L-shaped building that has an open southeast may struggle with extreme high or low energy levels.

If one must have an L-shaped building, then the wings should be the same size and preferably not go beyond a ground floor. And if one must have a U-shaped building, then the opening of the U should face either north, northeast, or east. If the opening of the U faces either the southeast, south, or southwest then the residents will have to brave the negative influences from those directions.

Trees, gardens, plants, and flowers

Neither tall nor short trees should be grown in the north, northeast, or east. Tall trees in those directions prevent the organic inflow of auspicious energies and the highly beneficial rays of the morning sunshine. An equal spread of tall and short trees in the west, southwest, and south is very auspicious because they help block negative influences from those directions. The total trees on your plot should not be an even number or a number with zero. Avoid having a tree directly in front of the main entrance of the house. Trees that cast shadows on your house between 9 am and 3 pm are inauspicious and should be avoided as much as possible. If cutting down a tree is absolutely unavoidable, tell the tree the day before doing so. You can say, "I'm sorry but owing to inevitable circumstances I am forced to remove you. Please forgive me. I will plant another tree of your kind at a suitable place and time." Having said that, give the tree some water. After removing the tree, within three months plant a tree of the same type and water it for at least three days.

Gardens are ideally situated in the open spaces in the north, northeast, and east, and the sitting benches in those areas should be in the west and south with a view to the north and east. According to *Vastu*, thorny plants (with the exception of roses or cactuses) have a negative influence and should not be planted on the house plot. Climbing plants should not be grown on the northern and eastern compound walls, they should be restricted to the garden. In your garden area, flowers are best situated in the west, northwest, and east but not in the southwest, southeast, or northeast corners.

Water reservoirs and wells

In ancient times, houses often had their own water wells and people would fetch their drinking and bathing water from the well daily. Nowadays, although most houses are fitted with piped water people still fetch their drinking water from a local store. So things have not changed much in terms of fetching drinking water. In the future, however, the need may arise to revert to one's own water well. And to that end *Vastu* strongly emphasises that any type of water cycle system must be in harmony with the five great elements and most importantly the course of the Sun. Harmonising water with Nature is achieved by positioning a well or any other water function in the northeast where the subtle quality of water becomes more auspicious.

The well should not be placed on the plot's northeast to southwest diagonal, as shown in the following diagram. The well should be located either to the left or right of that diagonal. The positioning preference of a well should be in

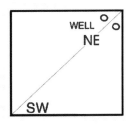

A well should not be placed on a plot's northeast to southwest diagonal. The well should be located either to the left or right of that diagonal.

this order: east, north, west, and then south. A well or any other water function should not be located in the southwest, southeast, northwest, or in the middle of the plot.

A swimming pool is best placed in the northeast of a plot. Sewage water systems should not be installed in the northeast near a drinking water system. Sewage systems can be placed in the northwest corner, the north, between the north and northeast, or between the south and southwest. In ancient Vedic culture toilets, and to some extent also bathrooms, were kept outside the main building. But if inside toilets can't be avoided then they should positioned avoiding the southwest, northwest, northeast, the four main directions, and the central area of a building.

An underground space without any construction on top of it is very conducive for meditation and spiritual practices, particularly in the northeast.

Compound walls

Vastu's rules on how to mark the plot boundary must be carefully considered. In *Vastu* it is customary to mark the boundary of a plot with walls while in Western countries plots are often bordered with fences or hedges. In general, a compound wall which has the same height and width on all four sides is good but border walls that are thicker and higher on the west and south side in comparison to the northern and eastern side is a much more auspicious arrangement. The colour of the boundary walls in the southwest are best dark grey or blue. The higher walls in the south and west prevent the Sun's infrared afternoon rays from falling onto the plot. The lower walls in the north and east allow not only the morning Sun to nourish the plot with its ultra-violet rays which are so important for health and vitality but also allow the inflow of auspiciousness from those directions.

Interior walls or fences can also be used to correct inauspiciously shaped plots. Disadvantageous corners can be fenced out by having inner and outer boundaries, the inner boundary being the an ideal square or rectangular shape that is conducive for containing, balancing, and utilising Nature's auspicious and inauspicious influences.

The digging of the hole for a compound wall or fence should begin on a Monday, Wednesday, Thursday, or Friday. Start the digging in the northeast and proceed anticlockwise to the southwest. The depth of the digging should be at least 90 cm. Then start constructing the wall in the southwest and continue anticlockwise to the northeast. The walls in the south and west should be thicker than those in the north and east. Take care that the walls in the southwest corner form an exact 90° angle. Walls in the north and east may be 30 to 60 cm high, and a railing may be added to it. In the north and northeast side of the wall there can be windows to provide light and air to the internal space. On the other hand, there should not be any windows in the south and west boundary walls.

Verandas and balconies should be located in the north or east of the house, and the floor should be a little lower than that of the main building.

Check Your Outside Placements

A tool shed

The most suitable place for an outside storeroom or tool shed is the southwest corner of the free space around the main building. The southwest corner should be heavy, and therefore tools and heavy metal objects are best stored in the southwest. The tool shed door should not be left open since negative forces congregate in southwest corners.

The tool shed should not have any doors in the southeast, northeast, or south. Its door should be lower than the doors of the main building. If one can't avoid windows in the tool shed then a window in the west side is best.

The roof, balconies, and verandas

The roof has two auspicious shapes: 1) The roof is equally raised in the middle with an equal height on all four sides, 2) the roof slopes facing the north or east with the south, southwest, and west on a higher level. A roof sloping to the south or west, which would position the north, northeast, and east higher than the rest of the roof, should be avoided because it may lead to serious health problems.

Terraces, balconies, and portals should be placed in the north, northeast, or east of the building. This positioning fosters health, wealth, and happiness.

A veranda is also best suited in the north and east sides of the house. This positioning protects the pure areas of the house in the north and east. The veranda floor should be a little lower than the house floor, and it should have a rectangular shape. The best places for seats on the veranda are in the south and west of the veranda. A swing on the veranda should rock from east to west. If applicable a veranda roof should be lower than the building roof, and should slant north or east. Pots for holding plants on the veranda should not be too big, and climbing plants on a veranda should be avoided. The north and east of the house are the best positions for a canopy. The southwest corner of the veranda should always be kept clear. The roof of the veranda should be 60 cm lower than the main roof, and a slope towards the north is auspicious. Avoid using dark colours for the veranda, light colours such as white or yellow are best.

Car parking

The direction best suited for car parking is the northwest, or alternatively the north or east. Avoid car parking in the northeast, south, or southwest of the building. If the garage or parking bay is located in the southwest, one can expect various car problems and repairs. If the parking lot is in the southeast, smaller problems and repairs are to be expected.

The roof over a veranda in the north or east should be lower than a roof of the main building.

A terrace should be located in the north, east, or northeast side of the house, avoiding the south or west.

The compound wall or fence around a plot in the east and north should be lower than the borders in the west and south. One should take care that there are no defects in the wall in any direction.

Summary of auspicious positioning on land quadrants

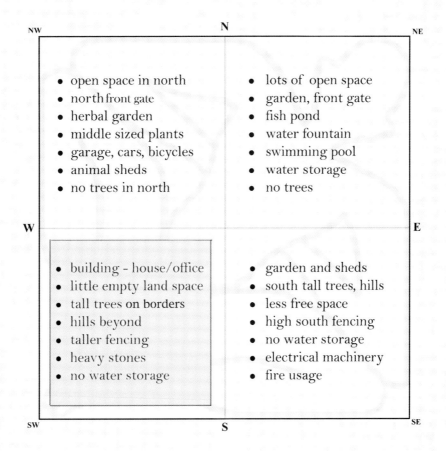

NW   **N**   **NE**

- open space in north
- north front gate
- herbal garden
- middle sized plants
- garage, cars, bicycles
- animal sheds
- no trees in north

- lots of open space
- garden, front gate
- fish pond
- water fountain
- swimming pool
- water storage
- no trees

W   **E**

- building - house/office
- little empty land space
- tall trees on borders
- hills beyond
- taller fencing
- heavy stones
- no water storage

- garden and sheds
- south tall trees, hills
- less free space
- high south fencing
- no water storage
- electrical machinery
- fire usage

SW   **S**   **SE**

Check Your Inside Positioning

Main entrance

The directional positioning of your main entrance is very important. The main entrance area is the 'face' of your house, the front door is the 'mouth' through which your house breathes in Nature's auspicious and inauspicious energies. Two windows, one on each side of the front door, are the two eyes of your house that increase good fortune. The protective threshold and frame around your front door are the lips of the face. The planets Rahu and Ketu, which are not known in Western astrology but play an important role in Vedic astrology and *Vastu*, provide protection all around (provided the house has good Vastu). Viewing your main entrance from the outside, Rahu rules the right side and Ketu governs the left.

The main entrance door should be bigger than all other doors.

A house or building with entrances on all four sides provides a healthy inflow and outflow of energies, particularly if the four sides face the main directions and the main entrance is auspiciously placed in the north or east.

Your house or office breathes Nature's influence through the front door. In Vastu, the positioning of the front door is most important.

The main entrance to the house on the left is in the north/ northwest segment and is thereby attracting financial gain.

Main Entrance Positions

Entrances on three sides of a house are auspicious if the main entrance is correctly placed in the east. Entrances on two sides of a house are also auspicious if they are positively positioned in the north and east. Only one entrance in a house is good if it is auspiciously placed in either the north or east. But only one main entrance in the west or or most south locations is inauspicious. The following diagram provides more precise details:

Degrees of positive and negative planetary influences that enter the various main entrance locations are depicted here on a plus 4 to minus 4 scale

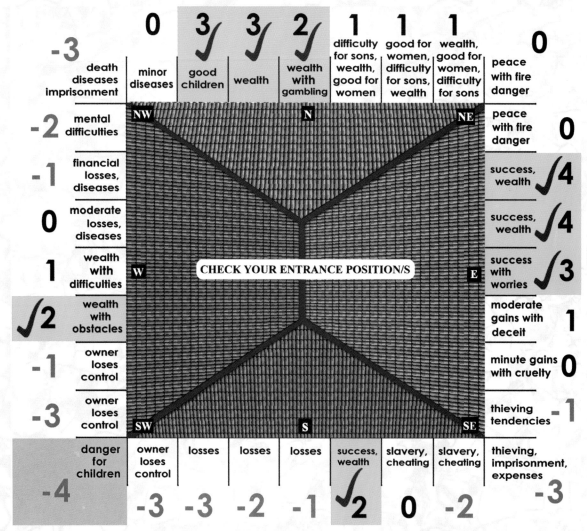

If the main entrance is in the east, the best place for a second entrance is in the west, and vice versa. If the main entrance is in the north, the best places for a second entrance is first in the east and then south. If the main entrance is in the south, there must be a second entrance in either the north or east to ensure that the south's negative influences don't get trapped in the house. Other good combinations for two entrances are east and north, west and north. The inauspicious combination of south and west, and a single entrance in either the south or southwest, must be carefully avoided. Always keep the main entrance to your home or office neat, clean, and tidy. All types of heavy things when left in the south and southwest are advantageous; but when left in the north, northeast, or east, or in front of your main entrance, they create inauspiciousness.

Check Your Inside Positioning

House centre

The centre of your house, known as the brahma-sthan, is of prime importance. As explained on page 11, the sub-creator of the universe, Lord Brahma, resides on the middle of the Vastu Purush's body in the centre of every building. He rules all the other demigods, personalities, and sages who are also present on the surrounding areas the Vastu Purush's body. Therefore, out of respect for Lord Brahma, the centre of a good Vastu house is left open, giving entrance to the maximum amount of light and air from above. This creates much auspiciousness. The same applies in Feng Shui wherein the life force in the centre of the house is called the Tai Chi. Therefore, having a toilet, kitchen, rubbish room, or bedrooms in the centre of your home disturbs the energetic centre, inviting various misfortunes. If occupying the middle of the house cannot be avoided (and nowadays that is the case with most houses), then use the middle area for more neutral functions like a dining area, living room, a spacious hallway, or a room which leads to other surrounding rooms.

It is an auspicious trait if the centre of a building's roof has an opening or window, allowing a good inflow of light and air to an empty space below. In the case of a window, it should be 60 cm higher than the rest of the roof. A centre-roof should slope towards the east and north. A pyramid-shaped roof construction in the centre of the house is ideal. The central floor of the house, if possible, should dip to ground level. The walls in the centre of the house should be white.

Lounge/living rooms

Lounge rooms are best located in the north or east of the house, giving preference to the east over the north. Rooms in the north of the house should be bigger than rooms in the south, and rooms in the north invoke auspiciousness if floor level is lower by approximately 30-90 cm. The door to the lounge is ideal in the west or east, avoiding the southeast and southwest corners.

Heavy objects in the living room such as cupboards and shelves are ideally placed in the south, southwest, or west. Furniture in the north or east of the living room should not be directly on the floor but should, if possible, be propped up around 2-8 cm above the floor. That furniture should be preferably light and hollow, and have square or rectangular shapes which are auspicious. Round, oval, or irregularly shaped furniture should be avoided.

Although in the ancient science of *Vastu* there is no mention of televisions, the principles that apply to the fire element (or electricity) are applicable to televisions on a basic *Vastu* level. Your television should not be in the northeast of the house or any room. A television located in the northwest of a room invokes excessive viewing, and in the southwest it is even more inauspicious. The ideal place for a television is in the southeast of a room.

In your living room, and other rooms, telephones are best located in the east, north, or southeast, avoiding the northwest and southwest. Religious pictures or motives, or pictures of a waterfall, create auspiciousness if located in the northeast. Avoid having depressive or sad pictures in your lounge rooms, and the walls should not be painted red or black but rather in light colours.

Lord Brahma, the powerful four-headed sub creator of our universe. The centre of all structures is reserved for him.

In the living room, one should leave more space in the northeast than in the other directions.

One should avoid having any heavy furniture or sofas in the northeast of the living room or study. If this cannot be avoided, there should be a distance of at least 20cm between the furniture and the wall. Sofas and other heavy objects are best placed in the southwest areas of a room.

Avoid hanging a heavy lamp in the centre of the living room, the ideal place is in the west. The middle of each room and the middle of an entire building is kept open and light to honour Lord Brahma, and therefore the centre areas in a house should not be weighed down with heavy objects. This *Vastu* principle corresponds to a similar Feng Shui rule: To obstruct the centre of a room or house is to block the chi, or vital energy point, resulting in a troubled living space.

Study

The study should be in the west, avoiding the northwest or southwest. Saturn rules the west with mostly an inauspicious influence. But Saturn is auspicious for learning because of Saturn's friendly relationship with Mercury which greatly facilitates a good education. Therefore Saturn in the west not only radiates the positive influences of Mercury (fostering brain activity) but also carries the influences of Jupiter (increasing ambition and curiosity). With this west positioning, the Moon contributes impetus for creativity and Venus enhances one's talents. In other words, all the creative aspects of studying, writing, and speaking skills are greatly enhanced through Saturn in a study positioned in the west.

While studying you should face north, northeast, or east. Position your bookshelves west, north, or east. Avoid keeping your books either in the northwest or in the southwest. Books in the northwest become too light and therefore may be stolen, lost, or not returned if lent out. Books in the southwest are too heavy and therefore there is the risk that they will never be read. Keeping pure water

A study with ideal positioning

Check Your Inside Positioning

in the northeast of your study creates auspiciousness. Avoid having a toilet near your study, but a bathroom is acceptable. The entrance/s to your study are best located in the northeast, north, or west. Windows in the east, west, and north allow the inflow of many auspicious influences. The most advantageous colours for the study walls are sky blue, light green, or white.

The kitchen should not be located in the northeast of the house.

Kitchen

The kitchen is one of the most important rooms in your house. The quality of the health and vitality produced by the cooks in the kitchen affects all the inhabitants of your household. The best location for the kitchen is in the southeast of your house, the direction that is ruled by the demigod Agni, the god of fire. The distinct function of the kitchen is the constant interaction of the elements fire and water, of which fire is the active principle. The second best place for the kitchen is the northwest. But the kitchen must never be positioned in the north, southwest, south, or in the centre of your house. Nor should the kitchen be located beneath bedrooms or toilets. These rules are of prime importance since non-compliance only invokes various misfortunes. When a kitchen is auspiciously placed, the intense use of the fire element in the kitchen bestows health and prosperity upon the householders.

In the kitchen, heavy things such as refrigerator, mill, cupboards, and so on should be placed in the south, southwest, or west.

A kitchen in harmony with Nature

VASTU - The Origin of Feng Shui

Position the stove in your kitchen in the southeast. The stove should never touch any wall. The distance between the stove and the wall should be around 9 cm. Electrical appliances in the kitchen should be put next to the stove on the southernmost wall.

The most auspicious direction to face while cooking is east; the next best option is south, and the directions to be avoided are north and west. Having an open area above your stove is auspicious. Avoid having an extractor hood directly above your stove because it disturbs the subtle flow and circulation of fiery energy required for auspicious cooking. Sufficient airing can be obtained with windows, or an extractor hole with a fan near your cooker (but not above it), or an extractor as part of a kitchen window.

Facing east while cooking generates a healthy energy from the Sun god.

The kitchen window/s should be in the east and/or west of the kitchen. Windows on opposite walls are ideal for air circulation. Auspicious entrances to the kitchen are the east, north, or west; the other directions should be avoided. A gas cooker should not directly face the kitchen's main entrance.

The kitchen sink is well situated in the northeast sector – the direction that is most ideal for all kinds of water containers. Grains, seasoning, spices, herbs, and other such items should be stored in the south and west. The refrigerator should be placed in the northwest, avoiding the northeast. If the fridge must be positioned in the southwest then it should be at least 30 cm off the wall, otherwise inauspiciousness will arise. The colours of the kitchen walls and floor should not be white or black but rather yellow, orange, brown, or red. If a dining/breakfast table is required inside the kitchen then it is best to position that table on the west wall.

If possible, do not cook with electricity or electromagnetic radiation. It is best to cook with wood or gas which are radiation free and do not in any way change the structure of your food.

In ancient India they regularly fetched sweet drinking water from a nearby well. But nowadays the quality of tap water in most Western countries is likened to a chemical cocktail. Hence the emergence of the massive worldwide multi billion dollar bottled water industry. Some concerned people are alternatively constructing their own wells activated into their existing systems, enabling them to enjoy pure bathing and drinking water.

Eating and kitchen utensils are best if made of earthenware or ceramic materials. Pots made of high-grade steel are also good. Aluminium pots and utensils should be strictly avoided.

Where drinking water is stored in the kitchen or elsewhere is very important. As mentioned earlier, water absorbs photons from sunshine and reflects or directly transmits them to human beings. Modern biophysics have verified that photons stored in water constitute a vital part of the human organism. Water absorbs the Sun's rays that contain valuable information, order, and food for your body. But water also easily absorbs negative influences that affect your psychophysical makeup, and sometimes to detrimental degrees. Therefore the best storage position for your drinking and cooking water is floor level in either the east or the north, avoiding any higher levels. However, if your water containers can only be stored in the southwest, a higher position is acceptable. Waste water should flow from the kitchen to a lower position towards the north or east, and should never flow towards the southeast, south, or west.

Electrical appliances are auspiciously placed in the southeast of a room.

In Vedic culture the kitchen is always kept impeccably pure. The cooks enter the kitchen only after fully bathing and putting on clean clothes. Avoid using a bathroom with toilet for washing clothes and towels that will be used in the

Check Your Inside Positioning

kitchen. It is best if this washing is done in a separate utility area for the sake of utmost cleanliness and auspiciousness in the kitchen. A correctly positioned kitchen where everything is kept clean, neat, and tidy enhances wealth and prosperity.

The ancient tradition in a Vedic kitchen is that the food is first offered to God out of gratitude and to get relief from the karma of killing different vegetables. During the offering, which can take less than two minutes, some powerful ancient Vedic mantras are softly recited while ringing a small bell. This makes the atmosphere in the kitchen very special. The cooks refrain from tasting any food until it is offered. This may sound difficult but for an experienced cook it is easy, since the benefits of regularly consuming sanctified food are immense. The general consensus among the many millions of people worldwide who follow this process is that they experience sublime material and spiritual benefits.

Pantry

The ideal place for a pantry is north of the dining room in the northwest sector of the house, or in the north or northwest of your kitchen if you don't have an extra room for a pantry. The pantry should not have a door in the southwest and should ideally have a window in the west and the east. The pantry walls should be painted mainly white, blue, or yellow. The cupboards should be placed in the western and southern sectors. In India it is customary to hang a picture of Lakshmi Narayana on the eastern wall of the pantry. Narayana is a name of God and His eternal consort is Lakshmi the goddess of all good fortune. In this way the store room becomes blessed with an abundance of food. Yearly provisions in the pantry should be stored in the southwest while food meant for daily consumption should be stored in the northwest. If you don't have a pantry or cellar, yearly provisions can be stored in the southwest of the building.

Inside your house the northwest sector should have windows. The northwest areas both inside and outside should not be used for storing heavy objects or unwanted scrap. These things should be stored preferably in the southwest or the south, keeping them separate from uplifting substances such as drinking water and food. The northwest on your land is ideal for an animal shed or sleeping place for pets.

Medicine and first-aid equipment are best stored in the northeast.

The kitchen should have a window in the east.

A pantry with containers brimming with food and cooking supplies creates much auspiciousness. Empty or near empty containers in the pantry obstruct positive energy fields.

A pantry with long and short term supplies correctly positioned

Food for daily consumption should be stored in the northwest of the pantry, and yearly provisions should be stored in the southwest. Inflammable foods like oils and butter should be stored in the pantry's southeast. And in the pantry's northeast there should always be a glass of fresh pure water.

Placing a glass or small container of pure water in the northeast of your pantry has the subtle effect of 'freshening' your food. Ensure the container is never empty. Food and other items connected to the fire element such as ghee (clarified butter), butter, oils, gas canisters, and other fuels should be stored in the fire god's corner of the pantry, the southeast. Avoid having empty fuel cylinders or food containers in the pantry since keeping all your cooking and fuel supplies well stocked creates an auspicious life giving energy.

Combined toilet and bathroom

A combined bathroom and toilet is best in the north with the toilet positioned 'between' the north and northwest, which is the most neutral area for a toilet. The rule here is that the toilet should not be aligned with any of the eight directions, particularly on or around the northeast. A bathroom/toilet should never be positioned in the centre, southeast, or southwest, and more importantly the northeast of a building.

A toilet in or just near the northeast is a serious Vastu defect because there lies the head of the Vastu Purush and the northeast is controlled by God, or Ishan. Vastu defects in the northeast mainly affect the male members of the

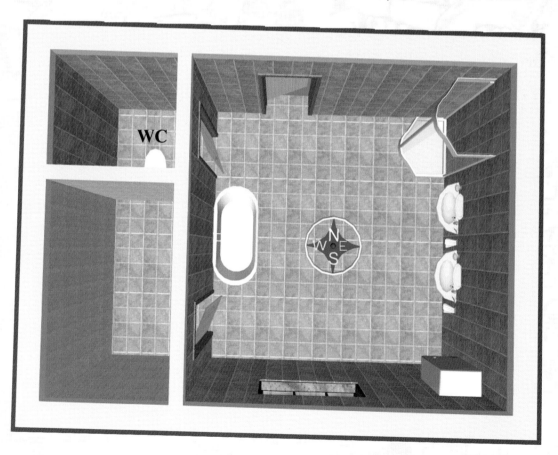

WC

An ideal bathroom with a separated toilet

Check Your Inside Positioning

house with physical or psychological problems to the head. The *Vastu* scriptures therefore strongly advise against having a toilet in the northeast.

Always keep the lid of the toilet and the door to the toilet/bathroom closed. This is very important. A toilet's negative energy should not be allowed to enter other household areas. The toilet should be positioned so that when sitting one faces either north or south. It is advantageous if the area around the toilet seat is raised around 30 - 60 cm above the floor. The toilet/bathroom door should be in the north or east, and a window is best in the east or north, or alternatively in the west. The toilet's water reservoir and taps should be in the north, northeast, or east but never in the southeast or southwest. The slope of the toilet floor (where applicable) should dip toward the north or east as should the drain for sewage water.

If you have an outside toilet, make sure it is not aligned with any of the eight directions. The most neutral locations are between the northwest and the north, and between the south and southwest. If an outside toilet can only be located in the northwest, there must be some distance between the toilet and the compound wall. Never put a sewage hole in the south. The best place for such a hole is between northwest and north. The old system of cesspools, or sewage holes, is hardly used. But if one does use such a system, placing the hole or pit in the northeast, southeast, or southwest must be avoided. The best place for a sewerage tank is west, or between northwest and north, away from any wall. The outflow direction of sewerage tank water should be to the north or west.

While sitting on the toilet one should not look towards the Sun in the east or west. The toilet should therefore be positioned to face either north or south.

Single toilet

A toilet that is completely separate from a bathroom is best. The best location for a toilet is 'between' the northwest and north which is a most neutral area. The general rule for a toilet is that it must not be directly aligned with any of the eight directions. In particular, the following directions should be carefully avoided: the northeast, either side of the northeast, the east, and the west.

In ancient Vedic culture toilets were kept as far away from the house as possible – at the end of the back yard. Even in Western countries only less than a century ago the same ancient *Vastu* principle was observed: toilets were kept at the bottom of the garden even in central London. But today we have clinical piped sewage systems that minimise the contamination. Nevertheless, such systems do not minimise the inauspiciousness because strictly speaking the

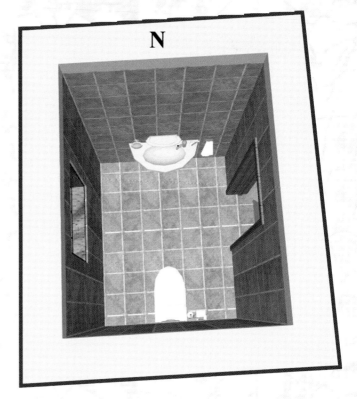

N

A guest should be hosted in the northwest of the house and should sleep with his/her head pointing west, or alternatively south or east.

toilet should not be in the house. But the inauspiciousness can be greatly reduced if the toilet is positioned between the northwest and north, a most neutral position, or between any of the other eight directions except the northeast. The cultural purpose of an outside toilet is to keep the total household living area pure because the toilet is where impure energy is flushed down the drain along with dirty water, and the inauspiciousness of this activity must be excluded from the rest of the house.

Results of sleeping with head pointing to a direction

The direction your head points during sleep has a significant influence. The magnetic axis of the body has its north pole at the head and the south pole at the feet.

Avoid sleeping with your head pointing north.

- **WEST - enhances wealth and fame**
- **SOUTH - invokes material happiness**
- **EAST - nutures spiritual knowledge**
- **SOUTHEAST - spiritual knowledge and material happiness**
- **SOUTHWEST - material happiness, wealth, and fame**
- NORTHEAST - spiritual knowledge, disease, and unrest
- NORTHWEST - wealth, fame, disease, and unrest
- NORTH - disease, and unrest

A bedroom with sleeping direction to the east

Check Your Inside Positioning

Bedrooms

We all spend a great deal of time in our bedrooms and so its position should be carefully planned. Bedrooms for children, adults, the house owner/s, and guests are ideal in various locations. The children's bedroom should be in the west, but can also be in the northeast which is unsuitable for adults. The southwest of the upper floor and alternatively the lower floor is best for the house owner/s. Grown-up married children are also well situated in the southwest. The air element in the northwest is constantly moving; and therefore guests – who are always coming and going – are ideally situated in reception rooms and bedrooms in the northwest.

The children's bedroom should not be in the southwest otherwise the urge for them to quarrel is increased. If a married couple sleep in the southeast, needless arguments will arise. Never have a bedroom in the middle of the house. A general guide is that the oldest members of the family should sleep in the southwest, and the younger ones in the west.

Bedroom Positioning
and the various influences from the eight directions

NW	N	NE
arguments but good for guests and children	restlessness and financial losses	emotional disturbances and illnesses, but not for children
W good for children and youths	inauspiciousness	bad health E
good for adults	good health	anger and quarrels
SW	S	SE

The bed, like the dining table, should not be placed under any beams.

The south is the ideal place for a bedroom. The best place for the children's bedroom is in the west.

The southwest is the best bedroom location for adults and the elderly.

The best positioning of rooms for ill persons is in the southwest or northwest.

Bedroom ceilings should not have any slope but be parallel to the floor. Some suitable bedroom colours are light pink, grey, dark blue, brown, or dark green. The bed should be in such a position that there is space to move on all four sides. Under no circumstances should the bed touch the northern or eastern wall. But the bed may be bordered by the southern or western wall, if you sleep with your head pointing south or west. If the bedroom is located in the southwest, heavy objects should be placed in the southwest of that room. For example, the bed could be put in that corner. If the four sides of your house are not parallel to the four main directions, then don't place the bed parallel to the walls but position the bed so that your head will point east, west, or south.

A bedroom book shelf is best in the southwest or west. A dressing table is best in the east or north. The west or east is a good place for a reading or working table. Electrical appliances connected to the fire element such as a television, heater, or open fire are best located in the southeast sector of a bedroom. Wardrobes are ideally situated in the northwest or southwest. The door to a bedroom should not be in the south. The north or east are good for small bedroom windows. The southwest corner of the room should not be left empty. An en suite bathroom and toilet attached to a southwest bedroom are best positioned in the west or north.

Bathroom without a toilet

A separated bathroom and toilet is best because this keeps the bathroom cleaner. The cleaner the entire house the more auspicious the atmosphere: cleanliness is next to godliness. A bathroom's specific purpose is to purify the body and therefore the toilet's negative energies are best kept out of the bathroom. According to the Vedic perspective, taking a bath is considered unclean since the dirt from one's body contaminates the washing water (unless one rinses off with 'clean' water after a bath). The cleanest preference therefore is a shower cubicle which is best positioned in your bathroom's east or north. If you have a big enough combined bathroom and toilet, you can (if possible) make it auspicious by constructing a separate toilet unit within your bathroom.

A bathroom that is not attached to a bedroom or toilet is auspiciously placed in the east or north, the best position being the east next to the southeast. This positioning gives access to the eastern morning Sun, provided there is a window in the east or southeast. The next best option for a bathroom window is the north. An attached bathroom without a toilet is best east or north of the bedroom.

The bathroom wash-basin should be in the northeast, or if that is not possible the next best alternatives are the east and north. Any bathroom electrical appliances such as heaters, blow-dryers, boilers, and washing machines are best located in the southeast. An extra dressing room in your bathroom is ideally placed in the west or south. Bathroom mirrors and doors should not be in the south but rather in the east or the north. If necessary, dirty laundry can be kept in the northwest of your bathroom but in a closed container. The bathroom sewage water should not flow towards the southeast or southwest. It is therefore advantageous if the bathroom floor is slightly sloped towards the east or north. Auspicious colours for the bathroom walls are white, soft blue, sky blue, and other such light and friendly colours.

Check Your Inside Positioning

Staircases

Stairs going up several floors or directed down to a cellar can either be inside or outside the building. Inside the building the stairs should never be located in the northeast. Stairs should not touch a wall in the east but should be a distance of at least 7.5 cm. The steps of the staircase should proceed from east to west or from north to south. If there are doors on the staircase, the upper door should be 2.5 to 22.5 cm shorter than the lower staircase door. It is inauspicious to have a continual staircase going down to the cellar and up through the upper floors. The total number of steps should be odd. Avoid positioning the staircase in the middle of the house, and the stairs should not begin from a storeroom, kitchen, or prayer room. The walls of the staircase should be light colours.

An outside staircase can proceed from the south, west, or southwest of the house. The steps should not be rounded off, they should be angular. The best position for a spiral staircase is the south-southeast, if the house is oriented towards the east or west. The best staircase position for houses oriented towards the north or south is west-northwest. The general rule for a staircase both inside and outside the building is always avoid the northeast.

Doors and windows

The arrangement of doors and windows is important. It is best if there is a window opposite the door to each room, if there is not another door there. If it is not practical to have two doors or a window and a door opposite each other, then there should at least be windows in the remaining directions of a room. It is recommended to have windows in the middle of the wall and not in the east-southeast, south-southwest, west-southwest, and north-northwest. Southwest rooms should have less and smaller windows and must not have three doors. In general, a door should be two or three times higher than it is wide, and the total number of doors and windows of a house should be an even number and not end with a zero. There is no rule for the number of windows and doors.

First floor

In a house with two stories the upper floor should be built in the southwest sector, leaving the north, northeast, and east sectors open. If the roof and floor have a slight slope toward the north and east, allowing rain water to flow towards the north, northeast, or east, this is auspicious. The first floor is ideal for bedrooms and studies for elderly family members, and should not be used for garbage or storage. The height of the rooms should not exceed the room height of the ground floor rooms. The first floor rooms should have windows in the east and north. A big window in the northwest is very good. The first floor must not have a balcony in the south or southwest. Balconies should be on the eastern or northern side, and should not be painted black or have any rounded corners.

A hand wash basin is best situated on a north or eastern wall.

The best place for a staircase is the southwest or south-east of a building.

Gates and doors should not be placed in the middle of an inside or outside wall.

There should be as many doors as possible opening towards the north and east.

On the upper floors, the number of doors and windows should be lower than the number of doors and windows on the ground floor.

Dining room

The west section of your house is ideal for a dining room, which should also be west of the kitchen. If the dining room cannot be positioned in the west, then alternatively it can be located in the south, north, or east. Avoid having a toilet next to your dining room, otherwise negative energies may enter your food. If the food from your kitchen crosses a staircase to get to the dining room, the auspicious energies of your food will be decreased. The door to the dining room should not be in the south or directly opposite the main entrance. A hand wash sink in the dining room (where applicable) should be in the east or north, avoiding the northeast, southeast, and southwest. Light colours should be used on the dining room walls. Preferable colours in light shades are blue, yellow, orange, or green. Pictures of Nature in the dining room create a conducive atmosphere for eating.

The most auspicious direction to face while eating is east. The north and the west are also good. But facing south should be avoided because that may induce quarrelling. The dining table should be neither round nor oval but should be square or rectangular and not touch any wall. Drinking water in the dining room should be positioned in the northeast corner or side of the room. This fosters the water's energy and purity in harmony with the movement of the Sun. Water is a very sensitive medium since it absorbs the most subtle information and energies from its environment and transfers it to the human body.

While eating you should avoid arguments or any discussion that produces anxiety, otherwise your natural appetite will decrease. If you eat in anxiety amidst disturbed surroundings, not only are the food's positive influences not properly assimilated by the body but the food absorbs the discussion's negativity that is subsequently absorbed by the mind. Avoid answering telephone calls during a meal because this may lead to indigestion. The *Ayurveda* asserts that the maximum enjoyment and benefit is gained from food when it is eaten silently. Talk during eating only if it is really necessary. Light music also helps relaxation and stimulates digestion.

Safe

Not many people nowadays keep lots of cash or extremely expensive items in a safe in their houses, they use banks and safe deposits. Nevertheless, where you keep small amounts of cash, cheque books, jewellery, a small safe is very important. The north is the most auspicious positioning for your safe and valuables because Kuvera, the demigod treasurer who is the sub-controller of everyone's cash flow, controls all the money you'll ever receive, and his influence comes through the north of your office or home.

If you can spare an entire room in the north of your house and you have sufficient valuables then place your safe in the most southern point of the room with the door opening towards either the north or east. This location is very auspicious. The safe should have a distance of about 2.5 cm from the wall. Avoid positioning the safe in the southeast and southwest corners/sides of the room.

Check Your Inside Positioning

The safe door should not be directly in front of a door from the north. This room should not have any doors in the southeast, southwest, northwest, or south. Windows are best in the north and east and they should be small and square or rectangular and positioned lower than in other rooms.

The safe should be put on a base and the surface beneath the safe should be flat and firm. Inside the safe no clothes or other things should be stored. Gold, silver, and other such valuables are auspiciously located in the southern portion of the safe.

The likely results from the positioning of one's safe or most valuable possessions:

North:	**Ideal for protection**
Northeast:	**Loss of wealth**
East:	**Neutral**
Southeast:	**Unnecessary expenditure**
South:	**Money slowly diminishes**
Southwest:	**Sudden loss of money or theft**
West:	**Miscalculation of money**
Northwest:	**Enormous expenditure**

Cellar/basement

Avoid putting a cellar in the south, southwest, or west. Excluding the northeast corner/sector, it is not good to locate cellars only in a corner of the building where negative energies may congregate.

Avoid putting a cellar beneath the south, southwest, and west sectors of a building. But if there is already a cellar in any of those positions, they are best used for storage only. A cellar beneath the east and north of the house is good, and a cellar in the northeast is very auspicious. Since the southwest part of any cellar is an area where negative forces may accumulate, no water should be stored there under any circumstances. Water stored in the northeast corner of a northeast cellar becomes imbibed with auspicious energies. It is inauspicious to have cellars underneath the entire building. But if that is already the case then heavy objects should be stored in the southwest, while the north and east should be used for lighter purposes. Light colours, mainly white, are best for the walls of a cellar/basement.

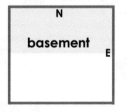

A cellar/basement should be in the north, northeast, or east of a building.

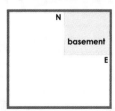 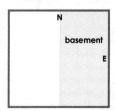

Heating

All types of heaters and fireplaces should be placed in the southeast of each room. And a central heating system is best positioned in the southeast of the whole building. The auspiciousness of the fire element is decreased in the northeast and increased in the southeast.

The Muladhara Chakra (root chakra) connects with and benefits the coccygeal nerves. The colour red is assigned to this chakra and its element is earth.

The prayer room

Even today in India, a large majority of householders dedicate one entire room for worshipping God. This room is called *pujaghar* and is best located in the northeast of the house, the direction assigned to God. The north and east are less suitable for worship, and the south of the house should be avoided. In the prayer room, the ideal place for the altar is the east or west so that the person looking at the altar or offering prayers can face east or west.

The prayer room should have windows in the north and east and have a source of light in the southeast corner. Agnihotras, or Vedic fire ceremonies, are best performed in the southeast of the prayer room with the person performing the ceremony facing east. Cupboards are best situated on the western or southern wall. Apart from the altar itself, take care that no heavy objects are put into your prayer room. Keep it light, neat, and clean. No valuables or a safe should be stored in the prayer room. Even if you don't have sufficient space for a prayer room or don't believe in any prayer it is still better to use the northeast area only for neutral purposes.

Colours and zodiac signs

In *Vastu*, the most auspicious and pleasing colours for the various areas of your house are chosen according to either the influences of the assigned ruling planets of the eight directions or your personal zodiac sign. The following shows which colours create the best harmony with one's zodiac sign:

The Ajna Chakra (forehead chakra) connects with the carotid artery nerve tissue. The colour assigned to this chakra is indigo and its element is water.

Aries:	coral red
Taurus:	white as milk
Gemini:	green
Cancer:	pink, white as pearls
Leo:	grey, ruby red
Virgo:	varicoloured, various greens
Libra:	concrete milk white
Scorpio:	coral red, pink
Sagittarius:	golden, yellow
Capricorn:	dark red, grey
Aquarius:	blue, pink or grey
Pisces:	yellow, shining white

Check Your Inside Positioning

The following table shows the directional sectors of your home and the colours that best harmonise the influencing planets:

East	Sun	bright white
West	Saturn	blue
North	Mercury	all kinds of greens
South	Mars	coral red, pink
Northeast	Jupiter	golden yellow
Southwest	Rahu	all kinds of greens
Southeast	Venus	silvery white
Northwest	Moon	white, light yellow

The Manipura Chakra (navel chakra) connects with and benefits the solar-plexus. The colour assigned to this chakra is yellow and its element is fire.

Colours have a significant physical and psychological impact on human beings. Modern medical science has proved that colours have a lasting effect on the individual functions of bodily organs. It is not just the eyes that react sensitively to colours, but our skin also differentiates and reacts to the exposure of different combinations of colours and light. In fact, colours are used in medical circles quite successfully for the treatment of physical and psychological illnesses.

The following table shows the acknowledged way in which various colours influence our nervous systems and chakras, or life energy centres, in the body:

Red:	**increases blood pressure, appetite, and enhances a family atmosphere**
Blue:	**counteracts the tendency of overeating**
Green:	**most ideal for operating theatres and doctor's premises**
Golden yellow:	**greatly enhances the quality of healthy foods**
Light colours:	**ease high blood pressure**

The more time and energy you put into arranging your colour scheme to suit your personal needs the more the quality of your living space is positively enhanced. Don't refrain from mixing or toning down colours according to what you feel is best for you. You could, for example, mix a greenish blue with white or greyish white and obtain a very uplifting effect. Or you could mix a little orange with such tonal backgrounds to compliment brown furniture, and so on. There are no limits to the creative possibilities.

A bedroom is a place of peace, and therefore the colours used there should not have a strong or heavy affect on you but should be soft and calming. The living room can take more dynamic and stronger colours. Rooms for babies should have light and bright colours because that is

The Anahata Chakra (heart chakra) connects with and benefits the cardiac nerve tissue. The colour assigned to this chakra is green and its element is air.

The Vishuddha Chakra (neck chakra) connects with and benefits the laryngeal nerve tissue. The colour assigned to this chakra is blue and its element ether.

what they see and feel best. Agreement with the daylight conditions are also of utmost importance when selecting wall colours. Rooms with very little daylight should be painted in light colours, whereas light rooms with big windows can more easily accommodate darker colours. If a room has only one window in the north, the colour of the wall should not be blue but rather warmer colours because only cold light enters from a north window (except, of course, in extremely hot climates). A room directly exposed to sunlight is best not painted in yellow or orange, and the ceiling of such a room should be white to reflect the light and warmth.

In a nutshell, your personal zodiac sign, health needs, room direction, daylight's quality and intensity, the room function, your decorative scheme, and your particular culture have to be carefully harmonised to achieve a living space that is just right for you and your family.

The Sahasra Chakra
connects and benefits the vertex chakra.
The colour assigned to this chakra is violet.

The Svadishthana Chakra (spleen chakra) connects with and benefits the spleen nerve tissues. The colour assigned to this chakra is orange.

Large size Sri Yantras increase the potential to attract money

Check Your Inside Positioning

This diagram shows the placement of inside rooms that best harmonise Nature's multifarious influences on the eight directional points in your office or home:

Summary of Auspicious Room Positioning

NW	N	NE
reception room, study, guest room, childrens bedroom, and toilet in north/northwest	main entrance, office/study, basement below, valuables storage, and reception hall/lounge	prayer/meditatiion, basement below, living room, and children's bedroom
W childrens bedroom, study, living room, storage, and dining room	open space for the ether element	main entrance, reception room, study/office, bathroom, and basement below **E**
adults bedroom, heavy storage, and recreation	dining room, staircase, bedroom, and heavy storage	kitchen, central heating, and electircal equipment

SW   S   SE

Defects that may Cause Cancer and Various Illnesses

Northeast defects may cause various cancers

In this section, we take a close look at cancer as a likely consequence of defects in the most crucial of all directions in an home or office – the northeast. We also take a brief look at possible consequential illnesses from defects in all other directions. According to strict *Vastu* principles, the northeast of your land should be an exact 90° corner, as part of an ideal square or rectangle shape, and should not be rounded or angled off. Nor should your northeast direction be blocked by other buildings, trees, or hills. The northeast should be the lowest point of the land and have clear open space beyond so as to allow the inflow of auspicious influences from that direction.

According to the scientific findings of Indian scientist Mr A.R. Hari, when a severe defect in the northeast combines with a defect in a different direction the combined disturbed bio-energy fields give rise to various types of cancer. Mr Hari extensively investigated the bio-energetic fields of many plots and buildings that had serious northeast defects. He scientifically measured and demonstrated that the disturbed bio-energetic fields of those premises were interacting with and affecting the bio-energetic fields of the residents. He also observed that the defective energies of the bio-fields were uncontrolled and chaotic in precisely the way that cancer in the body produces an uncontrollable division of cells that fatally invade body tissues.

Although the causes of numerous cancers are unknown to medical science, many medical experts are now attributing psychological disturbances to be a cause of various cancers. Aside from contributing factors such as stress, emotional grief, smoking, unhealthy food, and so on, exactly what brings on various psychological and mental disorders baffles medical science. According to *Vastu*, a significant contributing factor is the disturbed bio-energy fields arising from one's immediate surroundings, particularly when there is a serious combined northeast Vastu defect.

The quality control and bio-energy monitoring in every room of a building comes from the Vastu Purusha's head in the northeast sector. If the arrangement of a building disturbs the Vastu Purusha's mental condition, subsequently the psychological stability of the residents becomes disturbed. Just as cancer produces an uncontrollable division of cells wherein the intelligent communication between cells becomes increasingly chaotic, combined northeast defects disturb the bio-energetic fields of a building. The degree of exposure, one's psychophysical resistance, and one's good, bad, or mixed personal horoscope determine the overall extent to which one becomes psychologically and then physiologically affected. The longer the exposure the greater the chances of the disturbed bio-energy fields being transmitted to the psychological level of an inhabitant, and eventually contaminating a particular physical organism. On the positive side, having good Vastu in the northeast not only reduces the risk of cancer formation but has a calming and containing affect on a cancer patient.

Northeast defects particularly affect a male owner of the house and the male children in other ways. For example, a couple from Austria continuously tried to

Cancer begins at the molecular level in the aberrant dna of a single cell's nucleus and from there proceeds with a rapacious, all-out assault on the body.

Cancer is a resultant product of misusing Nature. The whole science of Vastu is the art of living harmoniously with Nature so that we can live free from unlimited diseases. All diseases arise from our ignorance of the workings of Nature.

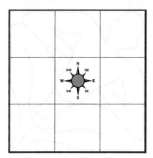

The Vastu Purusha, the lord in all buildings

If the northeast of a plot is rounded off or closed, cancer may develop in the breasts or lungs.

If the northwest, northeast, and east of a plot are higher than the west, southwest, and south a resident may develop cancerous brain tumour.

If a northeast defect combines with a defect in the southeast, breast cancer may develop.

If a serious northeast defect combines with a defect in the south or west, cancer of the uterus may develop.

If a serious northeast defect combines with a defect in the west or the southwest, kidney cancer may develop.

If a serious northeast defect combines with a defect in the west, stomach cancer may develop.

If the northeast of a plot forms an acute angle and in the west there is a hollow, cancer may develop in the head and throat.

conceive a child during a four year period, but were unsuccessful. The likely reason for their failure was that the northeast of their house was not open and free but was completely blocked by a bigger neighbourhood house. Just as the human body can't live without good oxygen, a house needs to breathe healthy influences from the north, northeast, and east in order to produce auspicious bio-energetic fields in the living spaces throughout a building. So after a certified Vasati consultant analysed their home, the couple accepted the recommendation and moved to an apartment with good Vastu in the northeast which was free and open. After one and a half years their first healthy son was born.

The resonance through which cancer manifests itself in a human organism, exerting its influence on the cells and prompting them to lose their equilibrium, is a combined northeast defect. The organ that is affected depends upon the location of the second defect. To that end the scientist A.R. Hari, after examining numerous cancer patients and tracing their condition to prolonged exposure to a particular combined northeast defect, compiled a list of those combined defects, as shown to the left.

We must always remember that whenever we experience good or bad health there are many contributing factors and having good or bad Vastu is just one. Because we spend most of our lives being exposed to the positive and negative energies of our immediate surroundings, namely our homes and offices, having bad Vastu is certainly a significant contributing factor.

If you find you have any of the above mentioned northeast defects in your home or office, try to correct them with the help of this book. If you feel you are unable to do so, contact an expert Vasati consultant (insist on Vasati, see at the back of this book). Certified Vasati experts offer a range of Vasati tools that can – in most cases – correct up to 98% of bad Vastu without the need of moving or reconstructing large sectors of your building (see page 94).

Northwest defects can spoil close relationships

Defects in the northwest lead to relationship problems. Relationships are enhanced when there is good Vastu in the northwest. Vastu defects in the northwest affect mainly women and (where applicable) the third son. Moreover, the Vastu defect of having a kitchen in the northwest, with a cooker in the northwest of that kitchen, ignites a tendency toward uncontrolled expenditure.

Southeast defects mainly affect women and children

Auspicious and inauspicious qualities in the southeast affect mostly women and children, and where applicable the second son. Southeast defects also invoke unnecessary quarrel, and in rare instances burns to women. But if the overall Vastu in the house is good and the kitchen is well placed in the southeast, Nature sends forth an abundance of health and wealth. Any kind of water structure in the southeast produces an inauspicious clashing of elements, since the southeast is ruled by the element fire. This defect affects the health of the mother, children, and particularly the second son.

Defects that may Cause Cancer and Various Illnesses

Southwest defects invite accidents and losses

Take special care of the southwest. If the southwest of the plot is higher, it indicates wealth and prosperity; but if it is lower, it invokes losses and accidents. Negative and positive Vastu in the southwest first affects the owner of the house, next the mother, and then the oldest son. Extensions in the southwest attract legal difficulties and debts. If construction changes are absolutely required in the southwest, the owner must personally oversee the work.

Defects in the east give rise to a decline in health

Defects in the east mainly affect the male children of the house. Openness and spaciousness in the east leads to health, wealth, and strong male children. Auspiciousness is created when the east side of the house has a veranda and the land in east is lower than the west. But if the land in the east is higher than the house, the male children are approached by poverty and bad health. Garbage, heavy stones, and junk in the east have a negative effect on the household wealth and the children. Eye problems occur if there is no open space in the east, or if an eastern veranda declines toward the west.

Defects in the west affect male children's education

Good and bad Vastu qualities in the west mainly affect the male children. The doors to wealth and prosperity open when the west of the house has a higher floor and a higher ceiling than the centre of the house. Inauspiciousness and suffering gravitate to the sons of the house when there is more space in the west of the plot than in the east. A door in the west that opens to the northwest invites lawsuits and monetary losses. And a door in the west that opens to southwest attracts diseases and unnatural causes of death.

Defects in north invite financial and health problems

Defects and positive aspects of the north mainly affect the women's health and the wealth of all others in the house. Open space and a low veranda in the north lead to wealth as well as happiness and satisfaction for the women of the house. If the plot is more spacious in the north than in the south, wealth is increased. However, heightened land in the north brings unhappiness to the women and a decline in the family's possessions. And losses are to be expected if there is any kind of garbage or hills in the north.

Defects in the south cause losses

The state of the south mainly influences women. If there is a lot of free space or land in the south, or if the southern parts of the house are lower than the rest of the estate, the women can expect economic setbacks and bad health. Additionally, the builder of the house will suffer from business losses if the south contains Vastu defects. Good Vastu in the south is to have heightened land in that direction which attracts good health. And a heightened room in the south of the house attracts health, wealth, and prosperity to the owner.

If there is a serious defect in the north-east and in several sectors around it, Leukemia may develop.

If someone with a good horoscope lives in a house with bad Vastu, the exhaustion of his/her good fortunes is accelerated. And if someone with a bad horoscope lives in a house with good Vastu, his/her negative astrological influences are reduced.

In the northeast of all buildings lies the head of the Vastu Purusha. If his head is disturbed by serious Vastu defects in that area then, to one degree or another, everyone in the house becomes psychologically disturbed, depending upon the severity of the northeast defect and the particular good or bad horoscopes of each individual.

Defects that may Cause Cancer and Various Illnesses

Vastu treats space in a house as a living being with consciousness and life energy. The subtle form of all living spaces is the Vastu Purusha, a being with a human body lying in a geometrical grid as seen in the background of the diagram below. The grid symbolises the strict geometrical spatial order, while the Vastu Purusha's shape represents consciousness and life itself. The Vastu Purusha mandala is the basic matrix in the *Vastu* ground plan. Its anatomy corresponds to the qualitative structure of space. Every grid cell of space possesses different qualities and is assigned to a different energetic aspect. The Vastu Purusha connects the living space of a building with its inhabitants. How the different spatial areas connect to your inner organs and any illnesses is depicted in the following diagrams: Check each of the directional areas of your office and home for Vastu defects and try to correct them as per the guidelines given in the corrections section. The advantages of having good Vastu in every direction can greatly enhance not only your health but so many other aspects of your life.

Bodily illnesses that may arise and organs that may be affected by bad Vastu in the eight directions

respiratory, lungs, digestion, joints, eyes, stomach, ovaries, womb, mental instability, female right eye, gullet, bladder, and psychosomatic illnesses	cancer, diabetes, liver, hip, lungs, gall-stones, nervous system, solarplexus, and skin problems	nervousness, liver, eye diseases, hips, sore throat, pancreas anaemia, itching, gall bladder, and body fat content
arthritis, ears, rheumatism, gall-stones, hair, weak knees, bones, teeth, and depressions	 N NW NE W E SW SE S	heart diseases, eye problems, circulatory disorders
bone diseases, teeth, and foot problems	measles, head, mumps, external sex organs, infections, flu, colds, left ear, muscles, blood, allergies, and prostate	eye infections, chin, ovary problems, skin diseases, cheeks, swellings, anaemia, liver, neck and kidney failure

Vastu and *Ayurveda* for Complete Health

According to the *Vastu* scriptures, there are two essential ways to maximise your health with *Ayurveda* and *Vastu*:

1. **Balancing the influences of the five cosmic elements**
2. **Harmonising your *doshas* with the five elements.**

1. Balancing the influences of the five cosmic elements

According to *Ayurveda*, the Indian science of natural herbal medicine and healing, the bodies of the hundreds of thousands of species on Earth are entirely made up of the five great material elements: ether, air, fire, water, and earth. Each of the five elements constitute essential bodily ingredients and functions as follows:

Ether:	**hollow spaces in the body, fine fields**
Air:	**movement, joints, breathing**
Fire:	**digestion, burning and metabolism of cells, blood**
Water:	**liquids, lymph, mucus (together with earth)**
Earth:	**bones, teeth, solid body components**

Just as you are what you eat, to varying degrees you are also made up of the energies of your immediate surroundings.

Vastu defects in each of the eight directions causes an imbalance of the five elements and can consequently give rise to various physical illnesses, as outlined in the following sections:

The ether and water elements in the northeast

In order for you to get vital exposure to the elements ether and water, the northeast point of your land should be lowered with open space beyond, and the building too should be open as much as possible to the northeast. If the northeast of your land is too heavy, unclean, closed up, blocked by a neighbour, or too high then the benefits of the elements ether and water are lacking. The same applies to the building. The possible consequences of this defect is a development of head and brain tumours and problems
with the body's water balance.

On the spiritual level, the northeast is controlled by Ishan, who is God himself, the controller of all other controllers. Good Vastu in the northeast is very auspicious for both spiritual development and maintaining good health. Inauspicious mundane activities performed in the northeast should be carefully avoided since in that area such actions quickly attract misfortunes and ruination. Therefore it is important to keep the northeast neat, clean, and tidy and use it only for auspicious activities.

The influence of one or two elements is prominent in each directional position of your office and home.

The air element in the northwest

The northwest of your land and property must be nicely balanced with sufficient air. Defects in the northwest of your plot such as heaviness, completely closed, no movement, or a lack of good air causes nervousness, breathing difficulties, lung problems, limitations of movement, and joint problems. Too much air in the northwest of your plot from a huge enlargement and entrances in that

According to Ayurveda, a meal is complete when it contains all six forms of taste: sweet, sour, spicy hot, astringent, bitter, and salty. All these tastes combined in one meal raise the digestive juices to their maximum level.

direction causes bodily weaknesses, loose joints, and flatulence. The northwest is controlled by the demigod Vayu who rules the air and wind, and his auspicious influence is felt through the right balance of and exposure to the element air.

The fire element in the southeast

To the southeast of your home and/or office lies the auspicious influence of the fire element. When fire/heat is nicely balanced we enjoy the affects of fire, but too much or too little fire/heat is obviously dangerous. Defects in the southeast such as too much water (an element which is opposed to fire), too many heavy objects, no space, or a neighbourhood blockage results in tendencies such as insufficient energy, lack of sexuality, weak digestion, kidney problems, a poor liver, and gynaecological problems. The defect of too much fire in the southeast such as enlargement, overly open space, and a southeast main entrance causes hyperactivity, insomnia, uncontrollable sexuality, influenza, organ inflammations, gynaecological disorders, and liver disturbances.

Therefore the right balance of exposure to the fire element in the southeast of your land and house is crucial. The southeast is controlled by the demigod of fire, Agnideva, whose auspicious influence enters a building that is correctly exposed to the fire element. Hence a kitchen is very auspiciously placed in the southeast of a building; and when combined with overall good Vastu in the southeast, good health, wealth, and prosperity are invoked.

The earth element in the southwest

The earth element's influence is strongest in the southwest of your office or home. A house with bad Vastu in the southwest facilitates entry to the inauspicious influences of the planet Rahu, the witch Putana, and Nairutva the king of the demons. Therefore the southwest should be short, blocked, raised, and heavy thereby increasing the auspicious presence of the earth element and strengthening the house owner's influence. A southwest that is enlarged, contains too much movement, is too open, spacious, and light gives rise to weak bones, chalky teeth, a frail body, and a weak muscular system.

2. Harmonising your doshas with the five elements

According to *Ayurveda*, your body is sustained by three *doshas* called *kapha*, *pita*, and *vata*. Each *dosha* is made up of two elements:

Kapha: (Earth and Water) stabilises and maintains the body.
Pitta: (Fire and Water) transforms and digests.
Vata: (Air and Ether) coordinates all bodily movements.

These *doshas* are not only active in human bodies but in animals, plants, fruits, and all living creatures down to the germs. Everyone's physical constitution is predominated by one of the three *doshas*; and accordingly, one's body

Vastu and Ayurveda for Complete Health

is designated as a *kapha*, *pitta*, or *vata* type. Health problems arise when a 'too strong' or 'too weak' imbalance arises from one or more of the three *doshas*. Understanding the *dosha* imbalance enables one to correct a health problem by carefully balancing the intake of food. In *Ayurveda*, all physical and psychic illnesses are traced to a particular imbalance of the three *doshas*. The following table provides a very basic guideline to help determine one's overall *dosha* type:

Physical attribute	Kapha type	Pitta type	Vata type
1) body frame size	thick	medium	thin
2) body weight	overweight	medium	low
3) appetite	slow - steady	good - excessive	variable - poor
4) mind	calm - slow	aggressive, intelligent	restless, active
5) physical activity	lazy	moderate	very active
6) speech	slow - monotonous	sharp - cutting	fast
7) sleep	heavy - prolonged	little but sound	poor - interrupted
8) emotional disposition	calm - attached	aggressive - irritable	insecure, unpredictable

Someone may be a *kapha* type in one way, *pita* in another, *vata* in yet another, and in this way each individual living creature has a totally unique *dosha* mix. In conjunction with the influence of the five elements in the eight directions, the following general principles provide important basic guidelines for each *dosha* type:

Kapha type

This type mainly lacks energy and vigour. But a *kapha* type can gain missing energies by spending more time in the northwest and southeast of an office or home. The southwest to the northeast axis heightens the *kapha* level and should therefore be avoided by *kapha* types. Also, *kapha* types are not well situated in the north and west.

Pitta type

This type must learn to say 'no', to be economical with energy. He/she needs stability and discipline which are promoted by using the southwest to northeast axis. The *pita* type shouldn't stay too long in northwest or southeast rooms because the fire element in the southeast and the air element in the northwest become strengthened. The southwest grounds the *pita* type whereas the northeast brings order, clarity, and spirituality. The cooling, protecting, and nurturing quality of the north is also favourable for the *pita* type, and the serenity of the west helps bring peace, harmony, and stability. Since the fire element is also present in the south, as it is in the southeast, a *pita* type should avoid long periods of time in the south part of the house. The power of the east and all other areas can be used by the *pita* type without further over heating of his/her fire element, just as all *dosha* types can do.

Vata type

This type primarily needs stability and a regular daily cycle. He/she has an already capricious nature and should therefore minimise use of the northwest or southeast since the dynamic energies from these directions may lead to an excess of *vata*. The *vata* type should make use of the northeast to southwest axis. The same is true for any other main axis which supports his/her constitution.

How the three doshas connect to the various directions:

In the northwest lies the air element that influences the *vata dosha*. If one's house or plot is defective in the northwest, one may expect *vata* disturbances. People with excess *vata* should therefore avoid prolonged dwelling in the northwest of a building. However, those with low *vata* will benefit in the northwest with improved movement and flexibility.

In the southwest lies the earth element that influences the *kapha dosha* in the body. Therefore the southwest area of the house enhances stability for *vata* and *pita* types. Kapha types should avoid extensive use of the southwest otherwise their *kapha* may become excess. Vastu defects in the southwest such as too much open space and lightness leads to *kapha* disturbances for everyone in the building.

In the southeast lies the fire element that influences the *pita dosha* in the body. Persons with too much *pita* benefit from not staying too long in southeast rooms, and those with too little *pita* should seek rooms in the southeast. If the southeast of a house or plot has too much water, a faulty area, or is too large the *pita* of the inhabitants becomes disturbed.

In the northeast lies the elements water and ether. Good Vastu in the northeast equally balances all three *doshas*. This most beneficial influence is called *sama-prakriti*. The northeast energies promote a balancing and equalising of all disrupted *doshas*. Vastu defects in the northeast therefore should be very carefully avoided.

The quality of the living energies in your office and home mainly depends upon how those buildings are absorbing the auspicious flow of energies from

Vastu and Ayurveda for Complete Health

the north and east. The more space your plot has in the north and east, the better the bio-energetic fields in the house. But those energies only find entry into your house if it has doors or windows to the north or east, and the east and north are clear and open. If the north is blocked by a windowless wall or another building, the house will lack important organic energies. If the east is blocked, there will be a strain on one's vitality, energy, inner drive, and will-power. The north energies are female and the east energies are male. Therefore a nice balance of north and east energies flowing into the house is very auspicious. Energies interact strongest in the northeast and therefore the northeast of the plot and house should be open, lightly designed, and clean.

If the north and east are lower than the south and west, the positive energies from the north and east are absorbed by your plot and house. Another very important aspect that affects the quality of a house's life energies is the position of the main entrance. The general rule is that an entrance in either the east or north gives entry to positive energies. And, as explained earlier, a south entrance is rarely beneficial, while the west is neutral. So if the east and north are defective, one should certainly take some corrective measures.

Vastu and *Ayurveda* are two branches of the *Veda* that are inextricably linked. *Vastu* serves to create an auspicious living space in one's home or work place and *Ayurveda* addresses the daily maintenance of one's physical health. To be completely healthy, *Vastu* and *Ayurveda* should be adopted simultaneously. Your health is significantly influenced by the Vastu qualities of your home or office because bio-fields in buildings directly interact with and affect the human bio-energetic field.

In other words, just as you are affected by what you eat daily, you are also affected by the daily multifarious qualities of your immediate surroundings, particularly the subtle spatial energy fields in your own home and office, the areas where we spend most of our lives. This influence occurs in the electromagnetic fields and on even more subtle levels. Vastu defects tend to affect the human body after prolonged exposure: it usually takes several years until chronic diseases are manifested. Positive Vastu aspects, however, have an immediate effect upon one's mental disposition, health, and energy levels.

The Ayurveda *assigns an ideal diet to every person according to his or her individual constitution. On principle it distinguishes between three types of constitutions which are connected to the elements:*

kapha - earth and water
pitta - fire
vata - air and ether.

How to Easily Remove up to 98% of Defects

When houses and offices are built without considering the harmonisation of Nature's multifarious influences, it is usually impossible to change certain physical attributes like the positioning and shape of the entire building. But there are many other defective features that can be changed either on the physical or subtle levels, as itemised below and explained in this chapter:

1. Correcting land shapes
2. Structural changes
3. Adopting behavioural changes
4. Adjusting the interior
5. Substituting or altering room functions
6. Balancing the five elements
7. Correcting with colours
8. Enlargement with mirrors
9. Energising with natural images
10. Using plants
11. Assigning crystals and gem stones
12. The placement of herbs and spices
13. Harmonising with ancient sounds, mantras, and music
14. Cleansing an old house with a Vastu-puja ceremony
15. The powerful Meru-Chakra
16. The Ultimate Vasati Pyramid
17. Vasati solutions for Vastu defects.

Defects in the first instance should be corrected with the recommended physical adjustments; but failing that, one should pursue the various subtle methods. For example, if your house has no window in the east, first explore the possibility of inserting a window. Otherwise, employ the more subtle method of using colours or symbols to strengthen the Sun's presence on that wall. But even more subtle and more powerful is correcting defects with *yantras*, the Meru Chakra, or the Vastu pyramid, or a recommended combination of these tools. The inauspiciousness of defects begins on the subtle level and so the subtle corrective methods are most effective. Carefully considered corrections communicate with your home's *prana* (life energy) and room energies and produce perceivable changes. Serious Vastu defects that can't be removed because of impossible physical alterations and unaffordable expenditure can easily be removed on the subtle level with up to 98% efficiency, as explained in the latter parts of this chapter.

A faulty land slope can be corrected by moving soil from one end to another. Any cost incurred will be easily recuperated by the auspiciousness gained.

1. Correcting land shapes and slopes

The most auspicious shape, positioning, and slope for a plot of land is as follows:

1. The shape is a 1:1 square
2. Four sides face the four main directions
3. The north and east are lower, open, and clear
4. The south and west are raised, heavy, and short

Rectangular plots up to 1:2 are also auspicious. But the more a plot's proportions exceed 1:2 the less conducive the plot becomes for containing, balancing, and utilising Nature's multifarious positive and negative influences. The best rectangle shape is a plot with a longer north to south

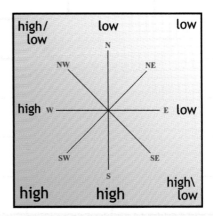

The ideal land shape and slope

VASTU - The Origin of Feng Shui

A plot with its corners pointing to the main directions is defectively positioned. The consequence is that success often escapes at the last moment.

dimension. The only auspicious irregular shape is a plot that is extended toward the northeast. Such a plot attracts wealth and prosperity. Expansions in all other directions are inauspicious. But even inauspiciously shaped plots can be corrected simply by fencing an ideal shape and using the excess irregular bits for gardening, playing, or parking.

A plot or house may be an ideal square or rectangular shape but if its corners point toward the main directions, the inhabitants will not completely succeed in their endeavours. The consequence of this defect is that success is so often close but slips away at the last moment (the opposition scores at the last moment or in extra time), or success is only attainable with a bad conscience. This is one of the inexplicable reasons as to why a person or team with less talent sometimes defeats a far superior opposition. In success and failure, Nature's higher controlling forces always have the final say. Therefore, a house or plot with its four corners pointing to the four main directions should be avoided, particularly by people in competitive business and sport.

In *Vastu* the shape of your land and building is crucial because cut corners or missing directions attracts Nature's negative influences:

A plot or building with cut corners or missing directions invokes various negative energies from Nature.

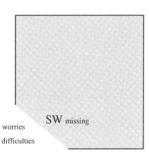

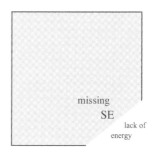

How to Easily Remove up to 98% of Defects

L-shaped plots and houses, as shown on page 43, are not good and should be corrected as far as possible by subdividing an auspicious shape so as to contain Nature's energies. If your land and house are not ideally shaped according to *Vastu*, and you can't change anything on the physical level, you can effectively counter the negative energies by employing some of the subtle methods mentioned further on in this section.

Structural changes

First try to alleviate defects on the physical level. For example, a misplaced main entrance in the south should be closed and replaced by a main entrance in the east or north. The inauspiciousness of no windows in the east and north can be corrected by physically putting windows in those areas. A water facility in the southwest or southeast should be moved to the north, northeast, or east. In this way defects should be corrected if possible on the physical level. But if such measures are not possible, or are too costly, consider installing a Meru Chakra or Vastu Pyramid.

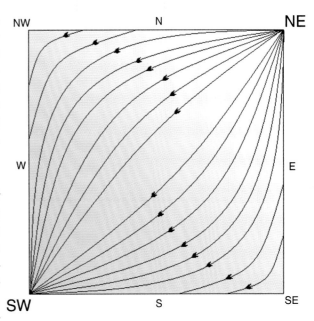

How Nature's auspicious energies flow from the north, northeast, and east to the opposite directions in a building and on a plot of land.

Adopting behavioural changes

Defects can sometimes be neutralised by altering usage. For example, an inauspicious house entrance in the south can be countered simply by not using it and alternatively using an already existing second entrance in the east and/or north. If you have two toilets and one is in the northeast, the inauspiciousness of using a toilet in the northeast can be countered by not using it. The inauspiciousness of a water function like a swimming pool in the southeast can be neutralised by not using it, or by using it for storage or any other purpose that does not involve water. A kitchen, bedroom, or toilet in the middle of the house is inauspicious but not using such facilities, if you have other alternatives, neutralises the problem on the physical level.

Adjusting the interior

Exactly where you position your furniture is very important. From an overall perspective the north, northeast, east and the middle of your house should be open and light while the west, southwest, and south areas are best heavy and closed. The same principle applies in every room. For example, the balance of energies in a lounge room are significantly improved if the middle of the room is open and light and the furniture in the north, northeast, and east are also light in colour and weight, while the furniture pieces on the opposite sides are heavier. Following this general principle, interior misplacements of furniture can be corrected and auspiciously placed.

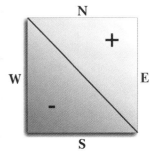

The north and east areas of the land, house, and each room should be light and spacious while west and south should be closed and heavy. This balances Nature's positive and negative influences.

Substituting or altering room functions

Swapping room functions can sometimes be an effective solution. For instance, if you have a bedroom in the northeast and an office in the south, which are both misplaced, swap them around because the south is ideal for a bedroom and the north is very good for an office. Once you know where different functions are best positioned in your house, you might want to start moving kitchens, bathrooms, and toilets around so that everything is auspiciously placed as far as possible. In most cases, however, to achieve 100% auspiciousness is either too expensive or impractical. If your Vastu is really bad and too difficult to change, then consider moving to a more auspicious house. Otherwise, even the most serious defects can be almost completely minimised with some of the powerful subtle corrective measures mentioned in the latter parts of this section.

Balancing the five elements

It is interesting to note that the human body, according to *Ayurveda*, consists of the five elements: ether, air, fire, water, and earth. And for the body to be healthy, the balance of these elements has to be just right. Similarly, in *Vastu*, your house is treated as the body of your body and therefore similar balancing rules apply to the five elements in specific areas of your office or home. This balance is absolutely essential for a healthy living space in your home. An imbalance in the elements can be restored by purposeful use of the five elements, as explained in the following examples.

Just as good health is experienced when all the body's five elements are properly balanced, a healthy living space is realised when all the five elements are directionally balanced.

NW air	N air/water	NE water/ether
E air/water **earth**	ether	ether/fire E
earth	earth/fire	fire
SW	S	SE

The auspicious influence of the ether element enters a premises through the northeast and east, as well as the centre of the whole building and the centre of each room. Openness and space, which is the ether element, is so important for maintaining good psychological health. Clutter and blockages in the northeast, east, and house centre as well as the middle of rooms chokes the ether element and creates a claustrophobic imbalance. If such ether deficiencies cannot be physically changed, you can improve the ether element's presence by subtle correction measures. For example, images of the sky and the stars give positive access to the ether element. Various harmonic sounds can also improve the ether element because sound is the inner quality of ether. And avoid outside unnatural background noises because they too influence the quality of the ether, or spatial element, in your office or home.

A south to north flowing river or canal to the east, northeast, or north increases success, wealth, and fame. But a river or canal either west or south is inauspicious.

How to Easily Remove up to 98% of Defects

The auspicious influence of the air element enters your home through the northwest, and to a lesser extent in the west and north. A blocked northwest leads to various health, movement, and relationship problems. You can correct an air element deficiency in the northwest both outside and inside your house by creating spaciousness and movement, and inhaling the breath of household plants.

The auspicious influence of the fire element enters your home through the southeast, and to a lesser extent in the east and south. Therefore a kitchen placed in the southeast is naturally auspicious. If you have bad Vastu in the southeast, if that direction is completely blocked (best is half blocked), then at least ensure that the general fire placement rules are followed. For example, heaters, electric devices, a stove, or even red fiery colours should be positioned in the southeast of a room. For heating purposes, best of all is an open fire in the southeast of a room since it radiates a natural fiery auspiciousness to the whole energy field. A natural exposure to the fire element is also obtained by bathing in the early morning Sun which is most beneficial for one's health. Nowadays, however, some people are becoming allergic to sunshine because the protective ozone layer is being eaten away by pollution. So bathe in the early morning sunshine, 15 minutes is plenty, but only after checking with a medical expert that your skin is not allergic.

The auspicious influence of the water element enters your home through the northeast, and to a lesser extent in the north and west. If you have bad Vastu in the northeast, strengthen the water element there by placing a small container of pure water (not tap water) in that area. Water stored in the northeast of a building (or room) with good Vastu becomes auspiciously energised. Moving water functions or pictures with waterfalls also energise the water element in the northeast. But avoid such usage in the other directions, particularly the southeast which is ruled by fire. Given that we are what we eat and that the human body is made up of mostly water, it is absolutely essential to consume nothing but the purest water.

The auspicious influence of the earth element enters your home through the southwest, and to a lesser extent in the west and southeast. If the southwest of your plot, house, or room is light and open it is bad Vastu because it gives a clear entrance to the inauspicious influences flowing from that direction. The southwest should be blocked and weighed down with the earth element. A deficiency of the earth element in a plot's southwest is strengthened by weighing down that area with tall trees, tall fences, raised land, outside storage buildings, and so on. Inside your building, a deficiency of the earth element in the southwest — and in the southwest of each room — can be strengthened with little space and heavy furniture. The presence of the earth element in the body is strengthened by walking without shoes on the earth.

Waterfall imitations or pictures in the northeast of a building attract good fortune and help rectify any Vastu defects in that most important of all directions.

VASTU - The Origin of Feng Shui

In Vastu there are many ways to correct disadvantages. But before buying or building it makes good sense to acquaint oneself with the basic principles of Vastu and then apply them as far as possible. The difference between having eighty five per cent and say thirty five percent good Vastu can make a significant difference to the quality of one's lifestyle at work or home.

Correcting with colours

Colours have psychological as well as energetic effects. Colours can be used very effectively to make various corrections. The following is a basic guideline on how certain Vastu defects can be corrected with colours:

- If your north is blocked or windowless, brighten it with green colours.
- If your south is too open, darken it with fiery and earthy colours.
- If your east is blocked or windowless, lighten it with sun colours.
- If your west is too open, balance it with a combination of airy and earthy colours.
- If your northeast is blocked, illuminate it with soft yellow colours.
- If your northwest doesn't provide sufficient airiness, broaden it with large white planes.
- If your southeast lacks energy, boost it with colourfulness.
- If your southwest lacks the earth element, reinforce it with earthy colours.

You can also combine with the above recommendations colours that are best for you according to your personal zodiac sign (see page 64).

The Vedic mantras inscribed into the Vasati yantras such as om namo bhagavate vasudevaya release powerfully auspicious spiritual and material energies into your building, driving away the worst of negative influences.

Enlargement with mirrors

Mirrors can be used simply and effectively to enlarge narrow, small, or odd shaped rooms and areas. Mirrors can enlarge a room that has missing auspicious directions. An inauspicious L-shaped area or room, for example, can be improved by placing a large mirror on the wall of a north, northeast, or east missing area, avoiding the opposite walls that reflect negative energies. The whole concept of *Vastu* is that Nature's positive energies from the north, northeast, and east should be given as much entrance as possible, and Nature's negative energies from the south, southwest, and west should be blocked. Where Nature's positive energies are missing, the positioning of mirrors improves such problematic areas by creating openness and space to the auspicious directions.

Energising with natural images

Images of Nature, particularly of running water, invoke the auspicious energies of the north and northeast. Such images are also effective in other directions provided the colours and motives harmonise with the directional qualities. Images of the sky and stars help correct the middle of a building that has no space for the ether element. Images of plants and trees help correct a building or room that receives no light from the north. Heavy images that show lots of earth help correct an inauspicious open southwest.

How to Easily Remove up to 98% of Defects

Using plants

Plants strengthen Mercury's influence and contribute a healthy breathing quality to the air. Since Mercury is the ruling planet of the north, plants strengthen a weak north and further enhance an already good north. Light plants are beneficial in the northeast, and big plants with much soil are best in the southeast. Ensure that you don't water your plants with tap water. Use only pure filtered water and your plants will be much healthier.

Plants inside a building promote health and a good living energy.

Assigning crystals and gem stones

Gems and crystals are mainly used according to their assignment to the planets that rule the eight directions. If your office and/or home has good Vastu, positioning auspicious gems and crystals is the icing on the cake. But if you have some bad Vastu areas, the beauty and healing energies in the shapes and colours of Nature's vast spectrum of crystals and gems will positively enhance deficient bio-energy fields. To determine which gems and crystals are best for your building, considering your building and personal horoscope, contact a certified Vasati consultant.

The placement of herbs and spices

Another correction system, or icing on top of the cake in a building with good Vastu, is the purposeful usage of herbs and spices in accordance with the various directions. Fresh or dried herbs and spices can be placed in little sachets on the wall or anywhere in the room. You can also use them as etheric oils. The natural aromas of herbs and spices connect us to Nature and thereby help us to remain calm and peaceful.

Harmonising with ancient sounds, mantras, and music

The subtle purification of living space through sound is known to all cultures. *Vastu* is a spatial science that empowers you to attract auspicious energies to your house, to give entrance to bio-energies that positively influence various aspects of your consciousness and daily life. Sound is most significant in *Vastu* because the entire Vedic culture is based on the use of various sound vibrations. Sounds and music, for instance, have a harmonising effect on a room's space, or ether, which is the subtle form of sound that determines a room's quality. Large parts of the *Vedas* describe the effects of sound, harmonies, *ragas*, and mantras on human beings and natural energies.

For example, the *Gandharva-veda* describes the affects of music on humans. This scripture vividly explains how harmonies or *ragas* generate specific moods by combining certain intervals and applying them in specific rooms. The intervals are summarised into a *raga* according to a room's proportions.

The *Shabda-veda* describes the effect of mantras on human beings and natural elements. Mantras are combinations of unique words and sounds which have profound spiritual and material effects. They contain keys that open Nature's most subtle mechanisms. When mantras and *ragas* are combined

Sounds of a sitar can effectively harmonize one's living spaces.

Harmony of Space – The Vastu CD
(Best selling CD. Available
through Vasati consultants.)

A Krishna Gayatri/Moon Vasati Yantra
This yantra invokes good fortune both
materially and spiritually when
positioned in the northwest.

A Narasingha/Mars Vasati Yantra
This yantra gives protection from
misfortunes arising from Mars/south
Vastu defects and/or a badly positioned
Mars in one's personal horoscope.

together they form a powerful combination. Mantras are therefore sung with specifically appropriate *ragas* and rhythms. To that end Vasati offers a powerful and immensely popular CD with totally authentic mantras and music that combine to put you and your house at ease.

Cleansing an old house with a *Vastu-puja* ceremony

Vastu recommends that one should never live in a house or occupy an office that has a bad history. The inauspicious energies of suicide, murder, insanity, bankruptcy, and fatal diseases can linger in buildings for a long time and influence the current residents. If you cannot trace the history of your building, cleansing the spatial energies with a *Vastu-puja* ceremony ensures that any lingering inauspicious energies are removed. The ceremony is performed by a qualified priest on an auspicious day and involves a colourful arrangement of mantra chanting around a small safe fire. Every room in the building is sanctified by incense, the sounds of musical instruments, and the chanting of auspicious mantras. If you require this service, contact a certified Vasati consultant.

Correcting with yantras

A *yantra* is a graphic geometrical combination of elements, colours, mantras, letters, and symbols used as an energy tool to insert positive influence on a room's energetic quality. The energies created by strategically positioned *yantras* replace missing natural energies. A *yantra* nurtures the energies of a room even if nobody is present. According to *Vastu*, each room is conscious and perceives everything in it. *Yantras* are vibrating images whose dynamics are experienced in the domestic or office spatial energy and give rise to a positive change in one's consciousness. The complex vibration of a *yantra's* image depicts and represents the relationship between space and time. As an image of the soul, a yantra reflects psychic and spiritual energies, and as a cosmic image it embodies specific universal energies and their controllers. The relationship between the inner space of soul and mind and the outer space of the universe is very close. The saying 'like the small, so the big' is here as valid as the saying 'like within, so without'.

Understanding the relationship between space and consciousness is the basis of *Vastu*, and *yantras* reveal that knowledge. The great *Vastu* science of building and living in a healthy, harmonious way sees space as an externalised reflection of the mind. Inner and outer space are not seen as separate but rather as constantly interacting. The outer space, i.e. our living situation, reflects our inner consciousness and our personal history, mirroring our past, present, and future. A Vastu master sees all this in a person's dwelling.

How to Easily Remove up to 98% of Defects

Yantras benefit us both internally and externally. Internal meditation on a *yantra* positively uplifts one's consciousness. The thoughts and feelings you have when looking at a *yantra* reveal much of yourself. *Yantras* directly mirror your consciousness and empower you with realisations on how best to change your inner world. Externally, *yantras* are used to produce the highest quality of energies in your living space. Correctly positioned *Yantras* in an office or home neutralise negative energies and to a large degree replace missing positive energies that emanate from Nature's major cosmic forces: the five elements, the ruling planets, and the controlling demigods. Each of these three powerful universal influences in the eight directions has their own *yantras* and mantras to correct debilitated spatial energies. The Veda Academy provides three main corrective *yantras*: planet *yantras*, Vasati *yantras*, and the room acupuncture *yantra* set.

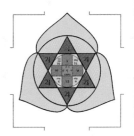

A Jupiter Planet Yantra
Placing this yantra in the northeast helps substitute any blockages to the auspicious influences of Jupiter.

Planet yantras

Each of the eight directions is ruled by one or two planets. If your house is defectively aligned with any of these planets, i.e. is open to the direction of inauspicious planets and/or obstructs the direction of auspicious planets, the quality of your life and house is diminished. For example, if your house is devoid of windows in the east and is therefore deprived of the auspicious energies that flow from the east, this problem can be rectified to a certain degree by positioning an auspicious Sun Planet Yantra on the eastern wall. This provides the auspiciousness of the missing solar energy on a subtle level. If your house has a blocked north, a Mercury Yantra corrects the problem since the north is ruled by Mercury.

The planet *yantras* either substitute the missing beneficial influences or block inauspicious influences that enter your premises from planets in the eight directions. Planet yantras can also be used to counter a negative planetary influences arising from your individual horoscope. High quality and authentic *yantras* for the planets Jupiter, Ketu, Sun, Venus, Mars, Rahu, Saturn, Moon, and Mercury are available through your local Vasati consultant

A Sun/Ramachandra Vasati Yantra
This yantra helps in the attainment of good health and spiritual progress when placed in the east.

Vasati Yantras

Apart from the planet *yantras*, the Veda Academy provides Vasati *yantras* that contain not only the auspicious influences of various planets but also the combined spiritual influences of certain avatars. A Vasati *Yantra* is simply a planet *yantra* with an added spiritual dimension, enhancing both material and spiritual development. Vasati *yantras* provide a broader application range than the planet *yantras* and have a finer effect. They are often used instead of the respective planet *yantra*.

A Jupiter/Vamana Vasati Yantra
This yantra helps one make huge leaps forward both spiritually and materially when positioned in the northeast.

A Mercury/Buddha Vasati Yantra
This yantra corrects north defects that block the auspicious influence of Mercury and the energies of the north that are essential for money and good education.

The original Sri Yantra. In Sanskrit Sri means opulence, and when positioned in the north or northeast this yantra attracts wealth.

Room acupuncture yantra set

Every room possesses four energetic key points known as *mahamarmas*. The qualitative ingredients of these points define the energetic quality of an entire room. Therefore placing heavy objects or walls on *mahamarmas* should be avoided. *Vastu* provides knowledge of the whereabouts of these points so that spatial quality can be positively influenced. To do this, Vasati has developed an authentic room acupuncture set. The set consists of four cheops-shaped glass pyramids with a *yantra* underneath each pyramid. The four *yantras* correspond to the energetic qualities of the four mahamarmas and establish a harmonic overall energy field. The combination of *yantra* and pyramid is special because the pyramids increase the power of the *yantras* and project them into the room.

A special advantage of this combined usage is that the four glass pyramids communicate with each other and establish a common field. Similar to the traditional Chinese acupuncture, the *mahamarmas* lie on the room's energy meridians and are assigned to a precise energetic room aspect. The Northern *mahamarma* represents the room's psychic-spiritual aspect. The southeast mahamarma is the energetic key point that connects with fire, warmth, and energy. The southwest mahamarma influences the stability and lifespan of the building, while the northwest energy point affects the quality of relationships, communication, and movement.

If the four pyramids are placed upon the mahamarmas, one will experience a vast improvement in the room's energetic quality. Other benefits are that Vastu defects are rectified and unfavourable room proportions are compensated. One can also use just one acupuncture pyramid to focus the *yantra's* power on a certain point from where the energy further spreads into the room.

The Sri Yantra

The Sri Yantra is one of humankind's most ancient symbols. For many millennia the Sri Yantra has been used to invoke good fortune, wealth, health, and as an aid for meditation. Nowadays, various research scientists have shown interest in this ancient Vedic *yantra*. The renowned American physicist Dr. Patrick Flanagan calls the Sri Yantra the 'king of power diagrams' and describes its energetic effect as seventy times greater than that of a pyramid construction. This means that a three centimetre Sri Yantra possesses a greater energetic effect than a two metre pyramid. The Sri Yantra's extraordinary energetic power depends upon its exact geometry. This complex geometry is the key to its effect and has interesting mathematical implications. In this *yantra* you find not only the 'Golden Section' but also parallels to the geometrical structure of the hydrogen atom

How to Easily Remove up to 98% of Defects

and to the ratios of its emission lines. In line with the original Sri Yantra, we (the international Vasati company) have precisely reconstructed the Sri Yantra's exact geometry and have given it a synergetic colouring.

The Sri Yantra is auspiciously placed in the north or northeast of a room or building. The flat side of the central triangle (with a dot in the centre) should face upwards. The Sri Yantra can also energise food, beverages, or other things. Simply place appropriate items on the *yantra* and let them stand there for a few minutes (the longer the better). The flat side of the Sri Yantra's central triangle should be facing east.

The powerful Meru-Chakra

The pyramid shaped Meru-Chakra is not only the Sri Yantra's three dimensional form but has much stronger energetic, favourable effects. The Meru-Chakra reorganises disturbed energies of living spaces throughout a building with verifiable results. When placed in the north or northeast of a room or house, the Meru-Chakra counterbalances a large percentage of energetic disturbances, disadvantageous room proportions, irregular house shapes, and other serious Vastu defects such as a toilet in the northeast.

One Indian physician has used the Meru Chakra in hundreds of problematic cases with great success. Most Vastu defects influence us on the subtle level, and therefore subtle energetic correction tools like the Meru Chakra produce powerful results in removing a large percentage of Vastu defects, particularly when combined with appropriate *yantras*.

The 24 carat gold plated Meru Chakra, **the auspicious three dimensional form of the Sri Yantra which attracts prosperity and good fortune from Nature.**

After many years of research, the Veda Academy of Germany has authentically reproduced the Meru Chakra in auspicious metals with a beautiful 24 carat gold plated finish with exact geometric measurements. The knowledge for the construction of the Meru Chakra was derived from ancient *Vastu* scriptures such as *Vastu Sutra panishad*, *Viswakarma Vastushastram, Matsya Purana,* and the *Stapatya-veda* which is a part of the *Atharva Veda*. Thus the Veda Academy's extensive research brings the ancient Meru Chakra's immense auspiciousness into your living spaces today.

The ultimate Vastu Pyramid

The most effective correction tool for the improvement of spatial energies is the Vastu/Vasati Pyramid. The Veda Academy in Germany, also known internationally as Vasati, (see details at back of the book), has authentically developed the Vastu Pyramid after extensive years of research and development. The Vastu Pyramid's unique effect is a synergetic combination of all *Vastu's* correction tools.

   The Vastu pyramid is a three-dimensional, relief-like representation of the Vastu directional *yantra*. In the centre is a transparent pyramid with a 7 x 7 cm basis, and combined with it are the Vastu Purusha and the Maha Purusha *yantras*. In the eight directions around the centre pyramid lie eight smaller pyramids with Vasati *yantras* beneath. The Vastu pyramid is best installed in the centre of a house or room or on another energetic key point. This powerful pyramid can correct Vastu defects to a high degree without any analysis. The Vastu pyramid's powerful effects penetrate problematic spatial energies in the following ways:

Yantras – A *yantra* is a graphic energy tool that has a lasting influence on a room's energetic quality with its geometrical elements, colours, mantras, and symbols. The three-dimensional combination of the twelve most important *yantras* in the Vastu Pyramid unfolds a powerful effect on the karmic level.

Pyramids – The effects of the *yantras* are energetically intensified and projected into the building with the help of nine pyramids.

Mantras – Inscribed in the stone relief of the base plate and positioned in the eight directions are auspicious mantras which neutralise inauspicious defects.

Vastu Purusha Mandala – In the centre of the Vastu Pyramid is a relief of the Vastu Purusha Mandala. The effect of this personal symbol of the ideal space is greatly intensified through the bigger central pyramid.

   Dedication Ceremony – The Vastu Pyramid can be installed with a traditional Vedic fire ceremony that activates its subtle energies. The pyramid thereafter becomes the energetic power centre of an entire building, supplementing to a large degree the missing natural influences required for a harmonious living space.

The effect range of the Vastu Pyramid

The Vastu pyramid equalises up to 75% of negative spatial energies and Vastu defects with an effect range of around 22 metres. But the most effective and far-reaching Vastu correction method is the combined use of correctly placed *yantras* with a Vastu pyramid and/or Meru Chakra. The huge advantage here is that the Vastu pyramid when combined with the right *yantras* and chakras can neutralise nearly all of a building's negative energies without having to probe into the specific nature of the defects. The counterbalancing effect of such a combined usage can be as much as 98%.

How to Easily Remove up to 98% of Defects

Vasati remedies for Vastu defects

Negative influences in a living or working space can be caused by one or more Vastu defects. Some defects are reduced by positive Vastu qualities such as a main entrance facing north, northeast, or east; windows facing an open north and east; and so on. As a general rule, however, defects should always be remedied with either physical alterations, a correct usage change, or a neutralisation by non-usage (like not using a toilet in the northeast).

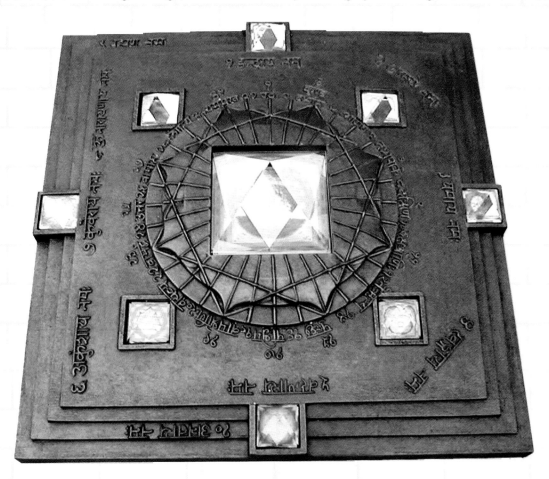

If none of those options are possible, Vastu defects, as indicated in the following chart, should be corrected on the subtle level with either the prescribed Vasati planet *yantra/s*, and/or the Meru-Chakra, or the Vastu Pyramid. The powerful Meru-Chakra is highly recommended for defect levels 4 and upwards. When seeking advice, always insist on speaking with a certified Vasati consultant, particularly if you have a few serious defects. The consultant can advise you through correspondence or with a personal visit and draw a plan of your building and precisely advise you why and how to best remedy defects.

Generally speaking houses and offices nowadays have several Vastu defects. Therefore the energetic levels in most houses can be greatly improved with a Meru Chakra in the northeast combined with one or two *yantras*, depending upon the specific defects. It is also beneficial to have a Vasati Pyramid in the central area of a building, a Sri Yantra above the entrance, and a Sri Yantra in the north. If several very severe defects coincide and the building has a bad history, it may prove better in the long run to take the trouble of moving to a residence that has relatively better or good Vastu.

Vasati Remedies for Vastu Defects

Vastu Defects	Defect Level	Possible Effects	Vasati Remedy
• Toilet, storeroom, or rubbish in northeast. • Northeast is completely blocked.	8	Lack of energy, learning difficulties, cancer, diabetes, liver disorders, and infertility.	• For a northeast toilet or a blocked northeast, place a Sri Yantra on the outside wall of the toilet/northeast area. A much more effective remedy is to put a Meru Chakra in the north or northeast. Since the Meru Chakra is a 3D gold plated Sri Yantra made with auspicious metals, it is many times more powerful.
• Main entrance in the southwest. • Southwest open with large windows. • Water, or extended land and/or house in the southwest.	7	Accidents, heart disorders, strong negative energies, fundamental anxieties about life, and mental problems.	• Place a Varaha/Rahu Planet Yantra in the southwest to counter the influence of Rahu, and put a Sri Yantra in the northeast. Best solution is to put a Varaha Yantra in the southwest and a Meru Chakra in the north/northeast.
• East is closed or contains any kind of clutter or rubbish.	5	Career obstructions, financial problems, problems with coral spine and heart.	• Place a Ramachandra/Sun Planet Yantra and/or a Sri Yantra in the east. Best is both the above and a Meru Chakra in the north/northeast.
• Four building corners point to the four main directions.	4	Disharmonious energy flow in the building.	• Install a Vastu Pyramid in the centre of the building.
• North is closed, contains a toilet, stored rubbish, or clutter.	4	Financial loss, lack of energy, weak immune system, frail bronchial tubes, and poor lungs.	• Place a Sri Yantra in the north. Best is a Meru Chakra, in addition to the above, in the north/northeast.
• Land or house extends to southeast or northwest.	4	Relationship problems, infections, breathing difficulties, depression, & diseases for women.	• Place a Parashurama/Venus Planet Yantra in the southeast. • Place a Krishna/Moon Planet Yantra in the northwest.
• Sleeping in the southeast.	4	Infections, weak immune system, and breast cancer	• Move sleeping area to southwest, otherwise, put a Parashurama/Venus Planet Yantra in the southeast.
• A wide open south with with large windows and/or a south main entrance.	4	Financial losses, aggression, and lack of energy.	• Place a Narasingha/Mars Yantra in the south and put a Sri Yantra opposite in the same room.
• A wide open west with large windows.	3	Delays, depression, degeneration, bone problems.	• Place a Kurma/Saturn Yantra in the west and put a Sri Yantra in the east of the building.
• Centre of building is obstructed.	3	A debilitated energy flow in the building.	• Install a Vastu Pyramid nearest to the centre of the building.

How to Easily Remove up to 98% of Defects

Avoiding clutter

Clutter arises in an office or home when the occupants give way to one of Nature's most powerful negative influences — laziness. When clutter is allowed to enter, clutter's many other associates also enter the building just as certain inauspicious living entities take birth in a dead body to devour it. Once clutter enters its negativity gets stronger and stronger until it becomes almost irremovable. Statistics and basic common sense clearly confirm that people in a clutter-free house or office always enjoy more productivity and a better quality of life. Whereas people who allow their living and working spaces to accumulate clutter nearly always attract various calamities.

This point about clutter cannot be emphasized enough. Clutter enters the human bio-energy field and inflicts disorganised thinking and subsequently one misfortune after another. But in an environment where there is absolutely no clutter, i.e. everything is neat, clean, and tidy, one's thinking and intelligence become clear and positively energised. This may be a common sense principle but it is also all too easy to let things slide into the precarious waters of clutter.

The most dangerous areas to allow clutter to enter are inside and outside the front gate, inside and outside the front door, the kitchen, the middle of the building, and the middle areas of all rooms. Clutter spoils the energies of even a building that has good Vastu, but the negative effects of a building with bad Vastu can be minimised simply by keeping the aforementioned areas clutter-free.

One Vasati consultant visited a house near London which had relatively good Vastu. The clutter in that house was so bad that the owner was powerless to do anything about it. The negative energies that were congregating around the clutter were inflicting a very strong energy of laziness upon the owner. After a powerful house cleaning session and installation of a Meru Chakra organised by a Vasati consultant, all the negative energies of the house were removed and thereafter every aspect of that householder's life was greatly improved. Avoiding clutter in the key areas of your living and working spaces is a basic principle in removing up to 98% of Vastu defects.

Just as every human being has gross and subtle pleasant and unpleasant attributes, Nature has a similar makeup qualities. She has gross natural disasters and pleasing beautiful features as well her subtle influences in the auspicious energies that emanate from the north, northeast, and east and her negative energies that emanate from the south, southwest, and west.

In Sanskrit man means mind and tra means to deliver. Mantras deliver the mind and one's house from Nature's negative energies.

Good Vastu Attracts Money

Your money, in the form of bank accounts and other various material assets, carries a powerful subtle energy field which is the result of your work (karma), your desires (kama), and your life energy (prana). In exchange for your work and time, Nature accordingly awards everyone with money to fulfil their desires and to enjoy life. Unlike days of old, making money nowadays consumes most of our lives, leaving very little time to think about much else. And if your money flow is disrupted, you'll probably experience a breakdown in almost every other aspect of your life. Just as the life energy of a living being is inseparably connected to its consciousness, the energy fields of money are intertwined with the mind, desires, and activities of all human beings.

The complex energy field of money follows the same *Vastu* laws as all other subtle energy fields. The following diagram shows how good Vastu in the eight directions of your office (or home if it is your office) affects the energy fields of your money:

Shops with streets and entrances in the north and east will flourish longer.

THE EFFECTS OF GOOD VASTU ON BUSINESS
arising from an auspiciously shaped office room, building, and/or land

NW
- good trading figures
- gains from low expenses
- accurate bookkeeping
- prosperity from creativity
- satisfied customers
- clear communications

N
- positive cashflow
- good planning and management
- real estate advantages
- long sighted banking
- solid securities

NE
- money comes auspiciously
- encouragement to use money for charitable or spiritual causes

W
- complete transactions
- good reputation
- skillful marketing
- communication success
- ability to investigate

- business openings

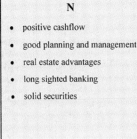

open space in the centre with natural light from above

- development potential

E
- legal stability
- innovation enhanced
- auspicious beginnings

SW
- profitable influence
- continuous cash flow
- personal strength
- secure savings

S
- responsibility
- continuity
- prosperity

SE
- abundant energy levels
- speedy transactions
- banking & property gains
- profits from stocks and shares

Retail sales flow more when customers face west or south and the sales person faces east or north.

Designing business rooms and positioning money transactions according to *Vastu's* basic guidelines can greatly increase business success. The following are some further important guidelines for business activities:

1. While conducting any money related activities, face east or north.
2. Cheque books, cash, credit cards, and valuable documents are safer if stored in the north or east of your office or business premises.
3. Financial affairs yield the best results when performed in the north of a building, and in the north of an office.
4. If the proprietor of a business conducts his/her work in the southwest of the premises, the quality of managerial influence is strengthened.
5. If you are negotiating the start of a new business, do so in the east sector. And when winding up a business, do so in the west.
6. Sequences of money related activities should be performed in a clock wise order.
7. Always keep the north areas of your office and business premises clean, neat, and tidy, and as far as possible open and light. This attracts positive flow of money energy from Kuvera, the treasurer of the demigods, the ruler of the north who controls everyone's flow of money. Installing the powerful Meru Chakra in the north of your business premises (or house) not only corrects any Vastu defects in that area but increases the success of business and monetary transactions. (There are many case files that verify money successes from the installation of a Meru Chakra.)
8. If the northwest or southeast of a business premises and/or land is completely blocked or cut, the flow of money is proportionately blocked.
9. If the southwest of a business premises and/or land is cut or too open, business stability is proportionately hampered.
10. Always keep legal documents in the north or east of your business premises and office.
11. If your shop has streets and entrances in the north and east, business will tend to flourish.
12. If shop customers face either west or south while speaking to sales persons, which means the sales persons are respectively facing either east or north, retails sales are more likely to prosper.
13. The cash register should be close to the southern wall and should open towards the north. If it is in the west, it should open towards the east.
16. A toilet in northeast is very inauspicious. And a toilet in line with any of the eight directions is also not good. Apart from the northeast, best is between the eight directions. But the most neutral place for a toilet is between the north and the northwest.

The cash register should be close to the southern wall and open towards the north. If it is in the west, it should open towards the east.

The following diagram shows the effects of bad Vastu on a business in the eight directions of an office building (or house) :

THE EFFECTS OF BAD VASTU ON BUSINESS
arising from the shape of an office room, building, or land

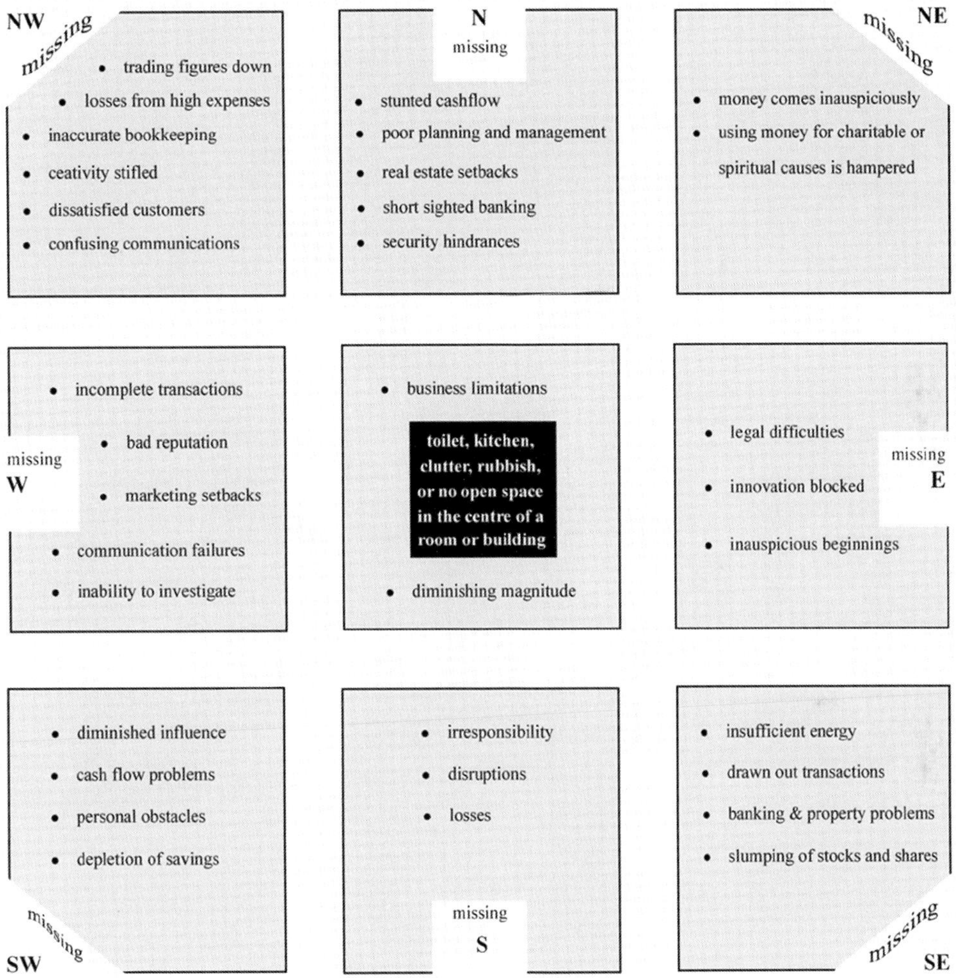

NW missing

- trading figures down
- losses from high expenses
- inaccurate bookkeeping
- ceativity stifled
- dissatisfied customers
- confusing communications

N missing

- stunted cashflow
- poor planning and management
- real estate setbacks
- short sighted banking
- security hindrances

NE missing

- money comes inauspiciously
- using money for charitable or spiritual causes is hampered

missing **W**

- incomplete transactions
- bad reputation
- marketing setbacks
- communication failures
- inability to investigate

- business limitations

toilet, kitchen, clutter, rubbish, or no open space in the centre of a room or building

- diminishing magnitude

missing **E**

- legal difficulties
- innovation blocked
- inauspicious beginnings

- diminished influence
- cash flow problems
- personal obstacles
- depletion of savings

missing **SW**

- irresponsibility
- disruptions
- losses

missing **S**

- insufficient energy
- drawn out transactions
- banking & property problems
- slumping of stocks and shares

missing **SE**

All the general principles of *Vastu* also apply to any room used for business. An office or retail shop with an entrance only in the south is likely to incur losses, unless the owner was born with a powerfully auspicious horoscope for earning money. In any event, any bad Vastu will accelerate diminishing of profits whether the owner has a good or bad horoscope.

In all our endeavours the ultimate hand in success or failure is Nature. It makes perfectly good sense to work in harmony with Nature's auspicious and inauspicious influences. All the ingredients of a successful business, as depicted herein, are greatly enhanced when all inside and outside aspects of a business premises are carefully positioned according to *Vastu*. The following diagram gives an overall summary of the ideal business usage and positioning:

IDEAL BUSINESS USAGE AND POSITIONING

NW
- guest reception
- communications
- acceptance of payments
- bookeeping
- creativity
- trading

N
- planning and management
- real estate affairs
- storage of valuables
- petty cash office

NE
- managements offices
- intellectual work
- no toilet in this area

W
- marketing
- public relations
- communication
- conference room
- project completion

clear open space in the centre of a room or building

E
- auspicious for project launch
- general offices
- legal affairs
- research and development

SW
- director's office
- top level meetings
- executive offices

S
- relaxation area
- security office
- cafeteria

SE
- manufacturing of goods
- heating and lighting systems
- processing offices

Divisions of Energy Fields in a Building

If you have the time and money to build your own office or home with maximum auspiciousness according to *Vastu*, you would need to find a suitable plot, build a house with an auspicious shape, divide the inside space into either 81, 16, or 8 energy fields, and then implement all *Vastu*'s guidelines for maximum auspiciousness. The 81 divisions of a building are generally utilised for big temples and palaces which require additional complex rules not relevant to residential buildings. The 16 and 8 divisions are sufficient for most offices and houses. Here we present the three main divisions of energy fields in a building, portraying a glimpse of the great science of *Vastu*.

Eight-fold division

The Vastu Ashtak Chakra is the division of a house into eight principal energy fields. In the centre lies the space of Lord Brahma, which is auspicious when left open for light and air. In Feng Shui, which has its origin in *Vastu*, the centre of the house is the life energy or chi and is given similar treatment. If the eight areas around the centre are used as depicted in the diagram below, the building attracts Nature's positive energies:

Vastu and Feng Shui require careful transplantation into one's own culture. At the building stage of a house you must carefully consider the significant influences of the materials, the plot of land, and the best time for building. The house and its inhabitants, therefore, are accordingly influenced by a certain mixture of auspicious and inauspicious directional influences.

NW	N	NE
guest room, living room, bathroom, food storage, toilet (nnw), children's bedroom	living room, safe, office, toilet (nnw)	drinking water, living room, prayer room
children's bedroom, dining room, study, toilet (wsw)	open space, air, light	bathroom (no toilet), guest room, meditation, kitchen, verandah
adult bedroom, storeroom, staircase	bedroom, living room, storage, toilet (ssw)	kitchen, central heating, electical appliances

W — E, SW — S — SE

On every plot and in every house there are auspicious and inauspicious places with positive and negative influences. They can be identified from the eighty-one fields of the Vastu Purusha Mandala and their 45 rulers, as depicted in the diagram on the opposite page.

Sixteen-fold division

The sixteen-fold division of a house incorporates more qualitative distinctions. Each section has its own individual quality that has compatible and incompatible usage. For example, water usage in the northeast of a house or land is compatible with Nature whereas as too much water usage in the southeast is incompatible. Incompatibilities give rise to various misfortunes whereas compatible usage brings good fortune. The quality of each direction depends on Earth's magnetic field, the gravitation field, the course of the Sun, the intensity of rain, the planetary influences, the five elements, and the controlling personalities of the eight directions who form the subtle background of all these interrelationships in Nature. The following diagram depicts the ideal usage in a building with sixteen divisions:

N

Living room, guest bedroom, staircase, and plants.	Child's bedroom, dining room, living room, study, toilet, plants, and entrance.	Living room, cellar, plants, office, safe, verandah, and entrance.	Openness, water storage, veranda, altar room, living room, salon, and cellar.	Prayer room, water storage, openness, cellar veranda, and living room.
Dining room, living room, toilet, guest bedroom, and food storage,				Entrance, cellar, prayer room, water storage, bathroom, plants, and verandah.
Child's bedroom study, staircase, living room, and dining room.		An ideal open courtyard creates auspiciousness.		Entrance, cellar room, small plants, prayer room, storage, bathroom, and veranda.
Bedroom, storage, toilet, and stairs.				Kitchen, bathroom, boiler, stairs, and dining room.
Adult bedroom, office, machines, and staircase.	Bedroom, storage, office, staircase, and toilet.	Bedroom, storage, and staircase.	Dining room, salon, storage, and staircase.	Kitchen, central heating, living room, and electric equipment.

W (left)   E (right)

S

Auspiciousness is created when the floors inside the building on the southeast, south, southwest, and west are higher than the north, northeast, and east. In this way (where applicable) water flows toward the east and north and not in any other direction. The central floor of the house, or if you have an open court yard which is most auspicious, should dip to ground level.

Eighty-one divisions

It is stated in the Vedic writings, the *Vastu Ratnakara*, that each of the eight directions is assigned to specific functions of a building. The division of a building into eighty-one energy fields is called Vastu Chakra. This divisional diagram provides a gross orientation on how best to divide and use a building. It is based on an ideally shaped square or rectangular building and divides it into eighty-

The Division of Energy Fields in a Building

one equal parts. The four corners of the Vastu Chakra point to the four second-ary directions while the four sides face the four main directions. The secondary directions comprise four squares, each forming rectangular corners, while the main directions are made up of five fields on each side. In the following dia-gram of the Vastu Chakra, each of the eighty-one divisions is assigned to a cer-tain personality or demigod whose influence rules the respective areas with a specific function and quality:

The areas of Ishan, Agni, Surya, Soma, and Brahma are most auspicious and should be used only for their recommended usage.

NW   **Kuvera**   **NE**

25 Roga	26 Naga	27 Mukhya	28 Bhallata	29 Soma	30 Rishi	31 Aditi	32 Diti	1 Ishan
24 Papa	36 Rudra	42 Ruddasa	43 Prithvi-dhara	43 Prithvi-dhara	43 Prithvi-dhara	44 Upvatsa	33 Upa	2 Parjanyai
23 Shesha	23 Shesha	42 Ruddasa	43 Prithvi-dhara	43 Prithvi-dhara	43 Prithvi-dhara	44 Upvatsa	33 Upa	3 Jayanta
22 Asura	41 Mitra	41 Mitra	45 Brahma	45 Brahma	45 Brahma	37 Marici	37 Marici	4 Indra
21 Varuna	41 Mitra	41 Mitra	45 Brahma	45 Brahma	45 Brahma	37 Marici	37 Marici	5 Surya
20 Pushpa Devata	41 Mitra	41 Mitra	45 Brahma	45 Brahma	45 Brahma	37 Marici	37 Marici	6 Satya
19 Sugriva	35 Indrajaya	40 Vishnu	39 Vivasvan	39 Vivasvan	39 Vivasvan	38 Savita	34 Savita	7 Brusha
18 Dwarpala	35 Indrajaya	40 Vishnu	39 Vivasvan	39 Vivasvan	39 Vivasvan	38 Savita	34 Savita	8 Akasha
17 Pitara	16 Mriga	15 Bhrigu Raja	14 Gan-dharva	13 Yama	12 Briha-kshata	11 Vitatha	10 Pusha	9 Agni

Varuna (left side)   **Indra** (right side)

SW   **Yamaraja**   **SE**

As indicated in the diagram opposite, the following places are considered to be inauspicious and should not be used for living: Yamaraja, Pitara, Dwarpala, Asura, Papa, Roga. At the same time these places should not be left open either. On the land mandala, it is best to plant tall trees on those places. Inside a building, the places of Pitara and Dwarpala may be used as store rooms.

In Vedic architecture the plan of a building is developed on the basis of the Vastu Purusha who is pictured as a 'person' lying on the floor of a mandala. He has sensitive and non-sensitive points on his body in respect of various house-hold functions, and therefore his sacred form is the placement basis of any architectural plan.

On the areas of Papa and Roga, a garage or other useful heavy structure may be built. The main entrance of the house should not be at one of these inauspicious places.

The Matrix and Mandalas of a Building

What is a mandala?

In *Vastu*, a mandala is a geometric form directed towards a centre, giving space a certain order, reflecting a natural order of the universe. A mandala expresses energy networks and spiritual relations in geometric and coloured symbols. Mandalas have strict geometrical meanings, psychological effects, metaphysical implications, and spiritual notions. They also represent physical energies, psychological emotions, spirit entities, cosmic principles, and spiritual personalities.

Auspicious qualities of various demigods and avatars are assigned to a particular mandala to give humankind beneficial access. Meditating on a certain mandala provides a subtle connection with the energy or personality behind the geometric form. A mandala may be square, triangular, hexagonal, or octagonal and may contain manifold forms and geometric nets depending on time, place, circumstances, and the personality whose energies are being conveyed.

Each of the five natural elements has a corresponding geometrical element that is symbolised in mandalas. In Vedic architecture, the elements are directly reflected in the external form of a building.

In the *Vastu-sutra Upanishad*, which explains the meaning of form, the natural elements are related to the basic elements of geometry. A line stands for the principle of separation and gives the original impetus for creation. A line therefore represents the activities of the Creator who manifests the variety of the world. Straight lines represent rays of light.

As depicted on the right, the *Vastu-sutra* allocates the vertical line to the fire element, the horizontal line to the water element, and the diagonal line to the air element. The circle around this cross represents the Sun. The figure created by these lines, that of a rhomb standing on its corners, is assigned to the earth element. Although the ether element corresponds to the basic structure of space, this element is generally not seen in a geometrical form.

In a mandala, the directions are of great importance. The fixing of directions is what establishes a clear relation between a mandala and reality. As indicated in the diagram below, the upper part is assigned to the north, the lower to the south, the left to the west, and the right to the east.

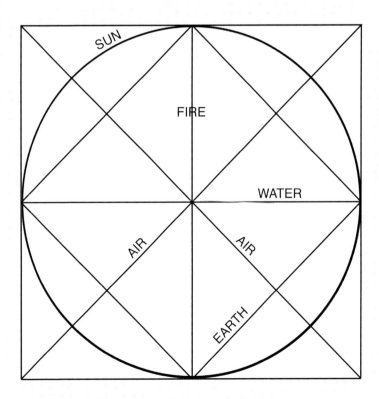

A geometrical expression of Nature's elements

The Five Fundamental Principles in Vastu

Separation as the basic principle of creation

In the diagram below, the upward triangle represents fire and the downward triangle represents water, while the hexagonal form represents the basic principle of attraction:

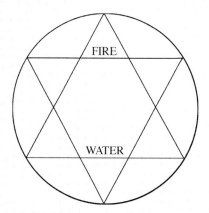

Hexagram representing an overlapping of the water and fire elements

The mandala of Vastu is the connecting pattern between humankind, Earth, ecliptic, and cosmos.

The line as a geometrical element symbolises a separation that corresponds to the metaphysical principle of the false ego, the basis of all material creation. From the original unity of spirit and matter, the principle of separation into internal and external manifests the diversity of the material world.

Mandalas have the same relationship to form as mantras have to sound. They are a visual access to the universe's spiritual energies and personalities.

Five fundamental principles in Vastu

1. Orientation of the plot and building

The axis of the plot and the building should run parallel to the main directions. Just as important is to determine the centre or the navel of the plot and building. The eastern direction, for example, has a special meaning, as do the northeast and the southeast.

2. Drawing the plan: the Vastu Purush Mandala

The Vastu Purusha Mandala forms the metaphysical plan of a building. It symbolises Earth's surface which is manifested by sunrise and sunset. At the same time it symbolises the elliptic and contains complex time cycles. The geometric application of these principles forms the foundation of a building plan.

3. Harmonious proportions and measurements

In the *Vedas* it is stated: If the measurements and the proportions of a building are perfect, the universe is perfect. Six different measurements are related to each other: Height, width, circumference, measurements of connecting lines, size of spaces, and gaps. The square is considered to be the perfect form, because in it the polar opposites become balanced.

The Sri Yantra, the mandala of the creation's power.

The Matrix and Mandalas of a Building

The following proportions between height and width are auspicious:

1:1	=	peace
1:1.25	=	strength, wealth, perfection
1:1.5	=	joy
1:1.75	=	health
1:2	=	grand impression

4. The six formulas of Vedic architecture

The first formula refers to the *aaya*, the product of the length and width of a building, from which, if multiplied by 9 and divided by 8, there will be a quotient and a remainder. A remainder of 1, 3, 5 and 7 is good whereas a remainder of 2, 4 and 6 is not good. The five other formulas are called: *vyaya*, *yoni*, *taaraa*, *bhavanaamshaka* and *grahanaama*. These will be elaborated upon in another book.

5. The character and aesthetics of buildings or chanda.

Chanda mainly refers to the structural aspect of a building and its rhythmic disposition. It refers both to the plot and to the vertical dimension. Special attention is paid to the contour of the building against the sky. *Vastu* distinguishes between six principal chandas or rhythms, which can be compared to the basic *ragas* in music: *meru*, *khanda-meru*, *pataaka-chanda*, *sushi-chanda*, *uddista* and *nasta*. These form 35 rhythms, and the same is true of building rhythms.

Vastu Purush Mandala

In the Vedic text *Mayamata* it is stated,

> "You should know that the Vastu Purusha has six bones, a single heart, four vulnerable points, and four vessels. He lies on the floor with His head towards the northeast."

The Vastu Purusha is positioned on the floor of the mandala and surveyed from east to west. The entire area of the mandala is divided into a total of 64 or 8 equal squares. Upon these squares reside 45 demigods, and their relative position to each other results from the division of the mandala. The picture of the Vastu Purusha corresponds to the plot where the house is to be built and symbolises the cosmic human being. The plan of the plot and the house should be in harmony with the form of the Vastu Purusha and his mandala.

Human existence is strongly influenced by three aspects:

1. The physical, social, and material environment
2. The inner mental thoughts of the self, intelligence, and ego
3. Energies from the universal and divine realms.

The divine realms enter our living space through the Vastu Purusha Mandala and connect with our physical and mental aspects by architecture. Thus by Vastu architecture we harmoniously connect our dwellings with the help of the mandala to the auspicious cosmic and divine influences. The Vastu Purusha

---

The Vastu Purusha, or the cosmic person, is not an anthropomorphism. It indicates that humankind are a reflection of a personalised universe and that the universe is a reflection of God. The concept of a cosmic person helps us to develop a relationship with Nature and the cosmos.

Vastu connects each energy and abstract principle with an expressive personality. In Vastu the aspect of personality is considered to be more encompassing because it is connected to consciousness, intelligence, and spirit.

According to Buckminster Fuller's definition of synergetics, the whole universe can be perceived as the densest package made of minute equal balls serving as a measurement for energy. These energy balls form patterns which resemble, depending on the number of balls, regular polyeders.

According to Plato, the five natural elements are represented by regular polyeders while in the Vedic Vaisheshika tradition the densest ball packages are used for the representation of the elements. Therefore the universe can be presented as a complex poly-dimensional structure of geometric elements.

The Vastu Purusha is completely awake when his head points to one of the main directions, and he sleeps when his head points towards the secondary directions.

Mandala varies depending upon the time, place, and circumstance and therefore each case is treated individually. Similar architectural concepts are applied in various Western countries. For example, Buckminister Fuller's concept of synergy is a three-dimensional system of energetic mandalas that cover a maximum structural complexity.

The *Vedas* state that the cosmos reflects a universal transcendental consciousness of perfect intelligence which creates and penetrates the world as an enlivening principle. This non-dual consciousness is called Brahman and his personal form is known as Vishnu. The whole cosmos manifests itself as the perfect mandala in which all elements of creation interact in perfect dynamics and harmony.

The Vastu Purusha Mandala is an embodiment of these cosmological principles, representing the blueprint of a perfect building. Consisting of a grid of squares from which all architectonic forms are derived, the Vastu Purusha Mandala organises space and is subsequently a symbol that encompasses the whole world.

Sakala Mandala

Traditionally, a distinction is made between 32 mandalas according to the number of squares used to form the square grid. The simplest form is a square that is not divided any further. This is called a sakala mandala and represents the mandala for the seat of an ascetic to organise the space around a holy fire. It is not used as a basis for the plot of a building. It distinguishes the qualities of the four main directions of the sky. In the north Soma, the ruler of the Moon, resides. The south is ruled by Yamaraja, the Lord of Death. The west is ruled by Varuna, the Lord of the Water. And Aditya, the Lord of the Sun, rules the east.

Pechaka Mandala

The second mandala consists of four squares and is called pechaka mandala. It rules over the demoniac forces and possesses secondary directions and therefore has an additional four qualities.

Pitha Mandala

The third mandala, with nine squares, is called pitha mandala or throne. There are mandalas with 16, 25, 36, 49, 64 and 81 squares. Other mandalas have even more squares.

Biggest Mandala

The biggest mandala has 32 fields on each side, containing a total of 32 x 32 squares, i.e. 1024 energy fields. On each side reside 32 demigods, who are identified with the rulers of the moon's 28 houses and the rulers of the four planets connected to the points of equality between day and night. This biggest of all mandalas is dominated by the movement of the moon while the earth mandala in the inner part is subject to the movement of the sun. Thus two different time cycles exist in this mandala with various courses, and they only overlap

The Matrix and Mandalas of a Building

from time to time. Such inequalities and imperfections form the basis of material reality. The cyclic movement of the axis of the earth is not in harmony with the cycles of the sun and moon. If everything were to vibrate in complete harmony, life would become paralysed in perfection and the manifested world would disappear into the unmanifested.

Manduka Mandala

The material world owes its existence to the aforementioned imperfection, which forms the basis of all astrological prophecies and astronomical calculations. When comparing the various cycles with each other, there is always a remainder. We are familiar with this remainder from the leap year and from the divergence between the Moon and Sun calendar. Without any remainder nothing would progress because all cycles would be equal. The space taken by the present time is located in the remainder of the past. In this way *Vastu* derives the living area from the remainder of the time cycles, indicating the complex relations between space, and the relationship between the various phases of the time cycles.

In the *Vedas*, the entire material universe is described as the gigantic body of God. It is compared to a cosmic person (Virata Purusha) on whose limbs we find the elements, planetary systems, demigods, and other living beings. This idea of a cosmic person was transformed by Vedic architecture into the form of the Vastu Purusha Mandala.

The centre of the mandala is regarded as the residence of the secondary creator and original demigod, Brahma, who is surrounded by other demigods. The eight directions are ruled by eight planets and powerful personalities. In this way the mandala symbolises sacred space and time's cyclic movements, encompassing the cosmos perfectly structured in time and space. For practical purposes, the mandala with all its subdivisions is transferred to the plot where you dig deep markings. By performing this process ritualistically, the architect forms a clear idea in his mind of the order of various parts of a future building.

The centre represents the heart of the building and forms the meeting point of all centrifugal and centripetal energies of the site. In monumental architecture the centre corresponds to an invisible internal column that reaches from the floor to the top peak. In temples, palaces, and even houses this is the place where the sanctuary or altar is located. In most residential houses the centre is often an open courtyard which lets air and light into the surrounding building. In the centre, the life force *prana* flows which – invisible to our eyes – is the vital principle of all life. As well as supplying spatial energies in all buildings, *prana* is the central life force that supports all other functions of life.

Although in general the Vastu Purusha's head lies in the northeast, he rotates clockwise one time around the mandala in the course of a year. The position of his head changes several times in that period. If his head points towards one of the main directions, he is completely awake. If his head points to one of the secondary directions, he is in deep sleep. Life on Earth goes through various phases of growth, maturity, decay, and re-sprouting. In relation to that, the best time

The presentation of Nature requires whole numbers only. The Vedic mandalas are two-dimensional projections of such space energy grids. Behind the numbers and their geometrical correspondences are energies and forces connected to consciousness and personality.

The demigods rule the directions but are not independent. They are known as demigods because they have been given administration over various aspects of the cosmos. They are empowered by God who is known as Ishan, the northeast ruler.

Vishnu is God while Brahma and Shiva are the topmost universal demigods. Lord Vishnu empowers Brahma to create and populate this universe (one of countless universes), and He empowers Lord Shiva to annihilate the universe while He Himself maintains everything.

Vishnu and Krishna are names of God referring to his transcendental form. Ishan means that God is the Lord of all other living beings, including the demigods. He does not perform the various functions of creation, maintenance, and annihilation directly but delegates these tasks to demigods such as Brahma, Agni, Varuna, Yamaraja, Vayu, and so on.

for starting construction is when Earth is vibrating with life and the Vastu Purusha is completely awake. This movement closely connects to the movement of the Sun, which is of prime importance for the cycles of life.

If the Vastu Purusha is asleep, one should not start constructing the house, and also the main door should not be put in during that time. However, since determining the most auspicious time to begin construction and other important events during construction depends upon so many other complex factors, it is best that these timings be calculated by an experienced Vedic astrologer.

The Vastu Purush carries out three different kinds of movements. In his steady form, his head is always directed toward the northeast. In his temporary form he changes his position with the rhythm of the seasons. In his daily rhythmic form he moves about 90° every three hours of the day, and then sleeps at night. In the first three hours of the day he faces east, and in the next three hours he looks to the south. In the next three hours he faces west, and for the last three hours of the day, before taking rest for the night, he faces north. The daily work at the construction site is determined by the daily movements of the Vastu Purusha, while longer cycles refer to the individual segments of the construction which may last for months.

The Vastu Purusha Mandala also represents a formula according to which the functions of a building can be determined in relation to the directions. According to Vastu, architecture harmoniously connects us to Nature in the form of the five great cosmic elements, the planets that influence buildings, the demigods controlling the eight directions, and to God Himself. The Vastu Purush Mandala projects all these influences upon Earth thus representing the programme or matrix upon which the microcosm of our dwellings are erected. The mandala for the construction of buildings, the planning of cities, villages, landscapes, and even the situation of whole countries is formed by the personality of Vastu, the Vastu Purusha.

The Vastu Purusha embodies the spirit of the deity of the building who carries the house and is responsible for its well-being. Various demigods who rule other aspects of life and the universe reside on his limbs. The architect planning a building should be aware of the individual entities, principles, and qualities assigned to them so that the structure can be constructed in harmony with those demigods and the respective rules of Nature. If these rules are violated, there is friction and disharmony which not only affects the building but the inhabitants too. Each human body is regarded as a microcosmic reflection of the complete universe. Therefore the body and house must be harmoniously connected to the cosmos by a matrix called the Vastu Purusha Mandala.

Creating Your Own Little Universe

When we create a living space with a house or office, we create our own little universe that entails all aspects, influences, and elements of the universe. In *Vastu*, the rules that apply to the entire universe also apply to our dwelling, place of worship, village, town, city, and country. How we abide by all the rules that connect us to the five great elements, the powerful universal controllers, and the planetary influences determines the quality of life we enjoy in our own little universe because Nature's laws are inescapable.

Vastu structures all dwellings according to the five elements and the natural order prevalent throughout the cosmos. The harmony of universal cosmic order is transferred to our own little living space. This function is fulfilled by the mandala which reflects the natural, metaphysical, mental, and spiritual interrelations in a geometric form.

The purpose of a house or office is not only to protect us from severe weather conditions but to help us live harmoniously and prosperously with Nature and the entire cosmos. The misunderstanding that Nature is an object to be conquered with any old type of buildings and factories has contributed to the serious ecological problems currently afflicting our entire civilisation. As long as we fail to understand ourselves to be part of a 'nature' that is not foreign to our own nature, we will continue regarding Nature simply as a manipulative, sense gratificatory object and suffer the consequences. But once we realise ourselves as an integral part of Nature – whose nature does not contradict our own nature – we establish with Nature a mutually beneficial and harmonious relationship.

Thereafter a building or village is not seen as just a defence against Nature's multifarious gross threats but rather as a manifestation of one's harmonious relationship with the whole living environment and the universe, a prototype little universe. A building becomes a manifest expression of our integration into the rules, time, life cycles, and moods of Nature. Houses, towns, and cities should not merely be creative expressions of egoistic emancipation from the rest of the planet but should be a microcosm that optimally integrates all cosmic, solar, earthly, and other natural relations. In this way the living spaces we create with our architecture are spaces that can either hinder or foster our higher values and purposes of life.

According to the Vedic understanding, creating our own living space is to create our own little universe. The microcosm of a living space reflects in a nutshell the structure and dynamics of the cosmos, Earth, and transcendental principles and influences that are beyond human perception. The relationships between Nature, Earth, and the cosmos are encompassed in the universe with its dominating forces: the natural entities, the demigods, and God. This holistic and very personal view of reality is clearly reflected in the foundations and techniques of Vedic architecture and is designed to keep human beings close to their transcendental origin. Vedic architecture reflects the complete personality of humankind, expressing the natural relationship between human beings and Nature.

Just as the harmony of Nature and the universe depends upon the overall balance of all the various influences, the spatial harmony in your home depends on how you contain, balance, and utilise all Nature's influences. This is the great science of Vastu.

Case Studies

Converting an Old Mill to a Conference Centre

How a somewhat inauspicious building called The Old Mill was converted into a relatively auspicious conference centre provides an instructive example for applying *Vastu* principles in Western countries. Although *Vastu* is best when applied to a new building, the following example shows how the application of certain *Vastu* principles can balance defects in almost any building.

The main building is U-shaped with the open side facing north, which is good. However, the eastern wing of the building belongs to someone else. The irregular plot of the new conference centre, which does not include the auspicious northeast corner, is another defect. The lack of complete ownership and the missing northeast corner can be balanced only by purchasing the whole property.

The Old Mill

Nevertheless, even with those defects the proposed conference centre has many auspicious qualities. For example, to the east of the building there is a stream that flows south to north and turns to the northeast. This corresponds to the location of the famous city Benares, in India. Vastu experts say that the fame, wealth, and spiritual significance of Benares are a result of its auspicious positioning near a sacred river. The downward slope of The Old Mill's plot from south to north is also very auspicious.

A river to the east flowing from the south to the north ensures success, wealth, and fame.

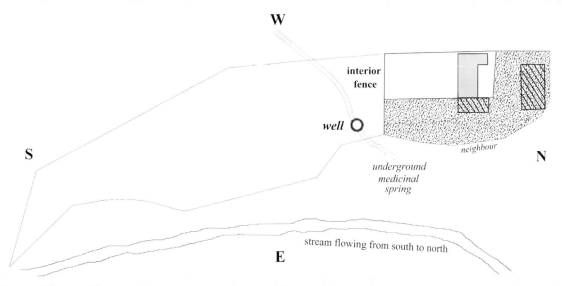

The conference centre plot with a neighbouring plot that blocks the northeast.

When Garuda is placed on top of a column in the southwest, protection is assured.

As shown in the illustration that distinguishes the two plots, the conference centre is disadvantaged since the auspicious northeast of the complete plot belongs to the neighbour. Other disadvantages are the long extension of the conference centre's plot toward the inauspicious south, and the auspicious north of the plot is blocked by the neighbour's plot. The south imbalance was corrected by separating the south of the plot with an interior fence. It is important that each division be used for a different purpose so as to contain and capture Nature's various energies. So the southern part was converted into a flower and vegetable garden, and the north section used for small buildings, garages, and a parking lot. The water well, as shown in the illustration, then became auspiciously situated in the northeast section of the south garden. The subterranean medicinal spring lying approximately forty metres below ground level also became auspiciously situated in the northeast of the garden and can be tapped for pure drinking water.

In the southwest of the garden, heavy and small sculptures, a summerhouse, an arbour, and a pavilion were erected. This corresponds to the principle to make the southwest heavy so as to get the right balance of the earth element thereby countering negative forces and entities that tend to gravitate to the southwest. A heavy pillar extending from the basement up to the roof inside the southwest of the building was installed to enhance further the earth element. A statue of Garuda was placed on the top of this pillar for protection. In this way the southwest became higher and auspiciously heavy.

In the southwest of the neighbour's house there is a high chimney which is good for his/her Vastu. But the same chimney for the conference centre serves as an obstruction to the east. A general *Vastu* rule is that the highest and heaviest objects of a plot and building should be in the southwest. Big changes to the southwest can adversely effect the owner, but if he/she personally supervises the construction then misfortune can be avoided.

The Old Mill building has one very good quality — the slope of the ground. In the north, the basement is on the ground level whereas the south of the basement is advantageously blocked. This sloping arrangement not only prevents the south's negative energies from entering the

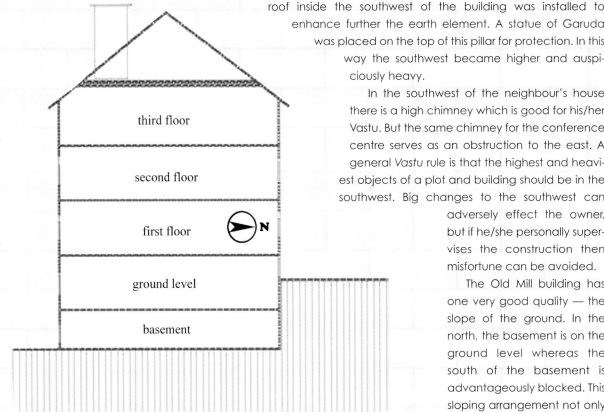

third floor

second floor

first floor ⊕N

ground level

basement

A view of the various levels in the conference centre

Case Studies

basement but allows the north's positive influences to enter, making even the basement auspicious.

The main entrance is in the south and this very inauspicious since it invites losses. Owing to strict building regulations, the main entrance cannot be removed. However, this problem was solved by creating an alternative main entrance for the residents and guests in the north part of the west side of the building. The southern entrance was closed and used only for decorative and emergency purposes. The *Vastu* rule is that if doors facilitating entry to negative influences can't be permanently removed, they should at least be kept closed as much as possible. Main entrance doors are best in the north or east, but for The Old Mill this was not possible. Nevertheless a main entrance in the west is better than in the south since the influences of the north side of the west can give rise to fame and wealth. A south facing door can also be corrected by changing the angle of the door so that it faces east. Another practical solution for a south facing entrance is to build a porch over the entrance and position the porch door to face east, converting a negative trait into a positive influence.

The following diagrams show the room positioning on three levels after the implementation of some significant auspicious changes:

When major changes are made in the south-west of a building, the owner must be present and oversee the quality control since losses and misfortunes easily enter through southwest extensions.

If the northeast wing of the Old Mill can be bought in the future, the auspiciousness of the conference centre will be greatly enhanced.

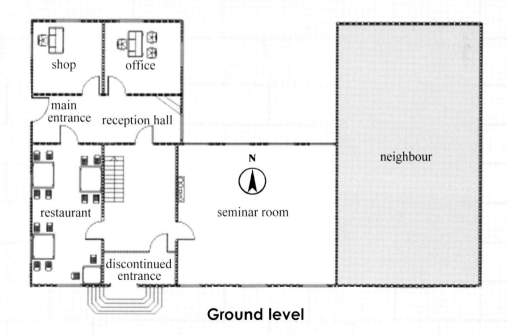

Ground level

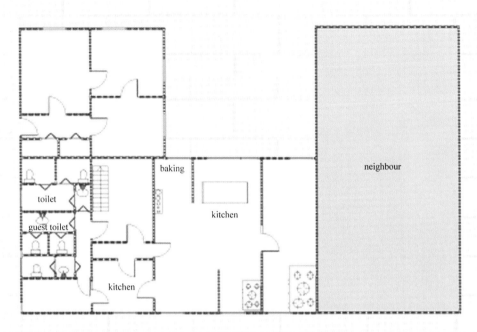

First floor

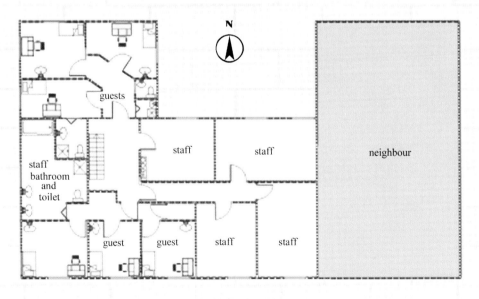

Second floor

Case Studies

The staircase for the building would be ideally situated in the northwest, leading from west to east. But this was impractical and so the staircase was moved from the southeast to the southwest, making way for the kitchen to be auspiciously placed in the southeast with its stoves along the east wall so that the cooks face east while cooking.

The baking area was positioned in the northwest, the realm of Vayu, to whom the air element is assigned. This influence is very beneficial for baking. On all the other floors the bathrooms and toilets were positioned in the west and all the toilet seats were correctly oriented towards the south or north.

The ground level was completely refurbished and the outcome was an impressive seminar room, a reception area, an office, and a restaurant. The restaurant is well placed in the west as is the office in the north, the reception, and the shop in the northwest. Great care was taken that the reception is oriented towards the west. The guest accommodation on the second floor was designed to position the guest rooms in the northwest. The heads of the guest beds point west while the heads of the inhabitants beds point east. This arrangement makes for mutually pleasant and prosperous relationships.

Despite many limitations during the refurbishment of the Old Mill, some very auspicious *Vastu* principles were implemented. Moving the main entrance from the south to the west, placing the kitchen in the southeast, locating the bathrooms in the west, arranging the guest and business rooms mainly in the northwest are but a few of *Vastu*'s many principles that greatly improved the Vastu of the new conference centre. Better still, of course, is to build a new house or premises from scratch, and this is reflected in the following case study.

A Vastu consultation for new home

Even building a new house according to *Vastu* principles can be difficult because in some countries there are stringent building restrictions and extreme climatic conditions. For example, a family was planning to build a new house in the Hunsrück area of mid-western Germany. So they instructed an architect to draw plans that included their own preferences and understanding of *Vastu*. The plan consisted of a basement, ground floor, and rooms in the roof level.

Although their plot is somewhat irregularly shaped, it has an auspicious downward slope to the north and east. A further positive trait is a street in the west. The plan incorporated making the most of the Hunsrück area's limited sunshine by locating the living room in the south. Those plans were brought to me to give a more complete *Vastu* consultation.

As depicted in the following drawings, I made many important changes. Instead of having the main entrance in the west, I placed it slightly west of mid north thereby giving the entrance access to the positive energies from the north. I then moved the bath-

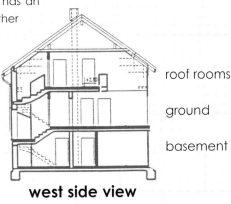

roof rooms

ground

basement

west side view

When reconstructing The Old Mill, only new materials were used. Vastu discourages the use of used materials since they may contain lingering negative influences.

Apart from implementing 'gross corrections' such as fencing a good shape, putting columns in the southwest, moving the main entrance, changing the angle of a door, and so on one should also use the recommended subtle corrections prescribed in the section: How to Remove up to 98% of Defects.

VASTU - The Origin of Feng Shui

south view

room and toilet to the other side, the northwest, and separated the bathroom and toilet to ensure cleanliness and auspiciousness. I moved the parents bedroom to the southwest, and reserved the northeast for the children. This was a good compromise for the roof rooms without having to change the plan in too much detail.

The centre of the house contained a large open space with a big south window the length of the floor up to the roof. This aspect would fill the house with light, warmth, and air circulation so that the residence of Brahma in the middle of the house gives entry to the maximum auspiciousness. In the south, a part of the ceiling between the ground floor and the roof floor was left open so that the living room would have a lot of open space in the south.

basement

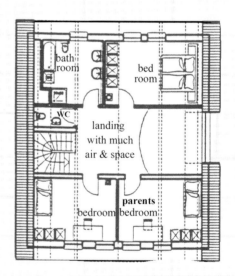

roof rooms

The position of the entrance and the kitchen, the northeast's purity, and having sufficient weight and protection in the southwest are important Vastu principles.

Some auspicious *Vastu* principles were adjusted but more needed to be done. A most important change was moving the kitchen from the east to the southeast, where it is ideally located. As a result the living room/dining area was moved to the south and southwest. The dining area was then auspiciously located west of the kitchen in the open south. The office was also well placed opposite the living room in the northwest. This freed the northeast to be used for meditation and prayer, which was very important for this family. A tiled stove west of centre to heat the big room in the south extending over two floors was replaced

Case Studies

with a better positioned heating system. The bedrooms for the children were placed in the west, the parents in the southwest, and the bathroom in the northeast of the roof floor.

By placing the garage in the southwest of the house, that direction became advantageously heavy. The house was located in the north of the plot in order to leave more space for a garden and terrace in the south to take advantage of the southern Sun. This conflicts with the *Vastu* principle to leave more space in the north and east than in the west and south. The reason for this compromise is that while one needs protection against the southern Sun in hot countries in Northern Europe any sunshine at all is a blessing. But this does not change the fact that the quality of the afternoon Sun is less than the morning Sun.

The planning of this family home exemplified a good compromise amidst stringent planning laws and difficult climatic conditions. *Vastu* principles are therefore implemented on a case by case basis. Only in very rare circumstances can one attain a completely ideal plot and then build a house entirely according to *Vastu*.

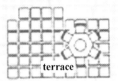

before

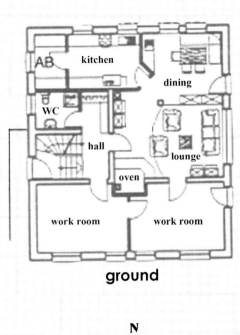

ground

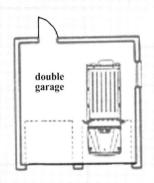

N

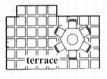

after

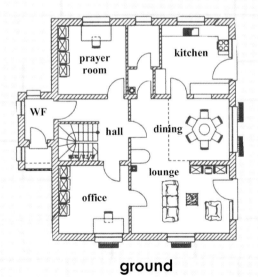

ground

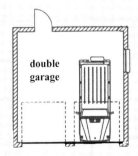

VASTU - The Origin of Feng Shui

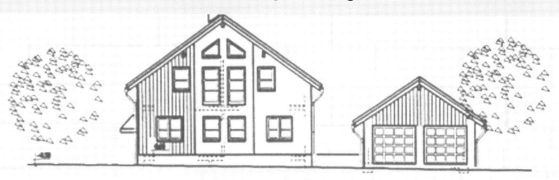

street view from the west of the new Hunsrück house

An architect's qualification

What is the use of living with negative influences in a palace or mansion? Is it not better to live simply in peace and harmony with Nature?

Vedic architecture entails complete knowledge of the structure of the universe, the movement of the planets, the elements of Nature, the ruling demigods, Vedic mathematics, astrology, and many other branches of knowledge. India's most famous ancient temples, palaces, residences, work places, villages, landscapes, and cities not only portrayed Vedic architecture's cosmic and spiritual dimensions but also the immense stature and irreproachable characters of India's greatest architects.

A master of Vedic architecture is known as a *sthapati* or *shilpin*. The Vedic tradition demanded from a Vastu architect an immaculate character. He was considered a scholar, poet, priest, and craftsman all in one. An architect who becomes deviated by envy, greed, lust, and anger paves the way to ominous inaccuracies and misfortunes.

The Vastu architect should have scriptural knowledge, practical experience, intuition, and an immaculate character.

Just as a poet weaves nets of dreams, an architect weaves the poetry of buildings. A Vedic architect is a creative artist who designs new creations on the basis of many intricate *Vastu* laws. He must know and thoroughly understand the practical application of *Vastu*. He must be thoroughly trained in mathematics, astronomy, astrology, landscaping, drawing, modelling, and woodwork. All that knowledge and practical experience are not sufficient for one to be a master. A spotless character is the essential empowering ingredient that enables an architect with deep intuition and a clear personal insight into universal relationships.

Acting in harmony with the laws of Nature leads to freedom while neither freedom nor happiness is gained by disregarding Nature or taking oneself as the only yardstick for one's activities.

Therefore the *Vedas* state: "The ocean of the science of architecture, which is without any light and is surrounded by darkness, is very big and difficult to cross. The many branches of architecture are impenetrable and can only be crossed if the sage has intuitive knowledge."

The *Vedas* also say: "A house built according to the laws of *Vastu* provides happiness, riches, health, joy, and peace while violating *Vastu* laws leads to unpleasant travels, failures, and disappointment. For the benefit of humankind, all houses, villages, and cities should be built according to *Vastu* scriptures."

Vastu and Geography

The science of *Vastu* is not only applicable to plots and houses but it is also helpful in understanding the history and special qualities of a city, country, island, and even a whole continent. Here it becomes clear that the natural laws upon which *Vastu* is based are of universal nature and not just anthropomorphic constructions of far-eastern superstition.

Japan, for example, is a small island which has achieved much considering its size. The Pacific Ocean is in the northeast which fosters Japan's influence and material development. The great length of its eastern side, the slight inclination towards the northeast, and the position of its capital Tokyo on the east side are big advantages. On the negative side Japan is exposed to constant earthquakes because she is surrounded by water in the south and west, some parts of her coastline are inclined towards the southwest, and the southeast corner is cut off.

Another good example is the United Kingdom, which also has had a tremendous influence on world history despite its relatively small size. The Atlantic Ocean in the west and the North Sea in the northeast are responsible for its powerful position. Her eastern side is so much longer than her southern side which enhances her power and influence even more. Her capital, London, is situated in the southeast of the country and is perfectly located on the magnetic north-south axis with its head towards the south. Cities with a big river flowing though or nearby are endowed with much auspiciousness, as with the city of London that has the River Thames flowing through her centre. The same is true of many other prosperous cities throughout the world. Many other qualities of London indicate Great Britain's powerful position.

The United Kingdom

N

If we also look at Germany from the *Vastu* perspective we notice that its capital Berlin is also located in the east. But as it is more in the north, the magnetic axis is contrary to that of Earth and so there is constant tension. Only in the north is Germany surrounded by water which is considered to be auspicious. The Alps are in the south and the main inclination of the country is from the south towards the north. The country is expanded towards the northeast which – according to *Vastu* – enhances wealth and prosperity. Its eastern side is noticeably longer than the south which indicates a powerful position which Germany has always maintained in history.

As for the Vastu of many other countries, this will be further elaborated upon in a comparative way in a future book on *Vastu*.

Germany

Japan

Vastu, Astronomy, and Astrology

Basic principles

Vedic astrology, known as *Jyotisha*, is applied in *Vastu* to determine the most auspicious time for laying a building's foundation, the commencement of the various stages of construction, and the size of land or house that is most appropriate according to an individual's horoscope. All astrologers agree that an auspicious or inauspicious birth time determines a person's life-long good, bad, or mixed qualities. For example, evil persons are born during heavy thunder storms and inauspicious planetary influences whereas pious persons are born when there are no such inauspicious disturbances. Similarly, the life-long attributes of houses and buildings are determined by their 'birth' time.

Astrology helps to harmonise certain characteristics of the building with the influences of the planets. For instance, the Sun planet, which embodies good health, rules the room which is reserved for the worship of God and meditation. The Moon, to which fame and honour are assigned, rules the bathrooms. Mars, the planet of wealth, mainly governs the kitchen. Mercury fosters studying, business, and a good character in the west side of a building. Jupiter rules the characteristic of respect and influences the room containing the safe or treasury in the north. Venus governs the ability of speech, verbal expression, and mainly rules living rooms, dining rooms, and bedrooms. Saturn stands for happiness and is assigned to store rooms and cow sheds. The planets Rahu and Ketu, which are not known in Western astrology, play an important role in Vedic astrology. Rahu rules the area right of the main entrance and Ketu governs the left. Their combined influence provides a protective effect all around the building. This will be described more in future publications.

Vedic astrology is based on a very sophisticated science of astronomy which is elaborated upon in Sanskrit scriptures such as *Surya Siddhanta* and *Siddhanta Shiromani*. A Vedic astrologer determines the planning or division of a building as a geometric pattern or mandala — the basis of house construction in *Vastu* — by carefully considering the influence of the stars, planets, and their time cycles and relating them to the various directions. *Vastu* divides rooms and buildings and designates beneficial or detrimental areas for certain functions whereas astrology focuses on the aspect of time.

In Vedic astronomy, the Sun, Moon, and other planets circulate on elliptic orbits covering twelve zodiac signs (*rashis*). Each sign consists of two star constellations called *naksatras*, making 27 *naksatras* in all, each of which has four parts or *padas*. Consequently each sign of the zodiac has an angle of 30°, each *naksatra* 13°20', and each *pada* 3°20'.

Signs of the zodiac

The following illustration shows the position of the signs, stars, angles, and names of the demigods who rule the respective stars. Although there are millions of stars in our universe, only 27 *nakshatras* are meaningful because Earth and the Sun are moving in their sphere of influence. Uranus, Neptune, and Pluto are ignored in Vedic astrology because their influence on human life is considered negligible owing to their great distance.

The gross and subtle forces of Nature that arise from planetary influences are indeed powerful, in fact insurmountable. But if one knows the art of living in harmony with Nature one is not affected just as a kitten is not harmed by the jaws of its mother.

The forces of Mother Nature are completely beyond our control. But those who live according to Nature's laws are never harmed by Nature and can even influence the workings of Nature.

A Vedic horoscope consists of five parts called *pancanga*: respecting date, star, *thiti* (phase of the Moon), yoga (various constellations of the Sun, Moon, and planets) and *karana* (effects of the week in relation to the *thitis* and various constellations).

	1		**2**	
12	Meen = **PISCES** 331 – 360° P. Bhadrapad-4 U. Bhadrapad, Revati	Mesha = **ARIES** 0 – 30° Aswini, Bharani Kritik 1	Rishab = **TAURUS** 31 – 60° Kirtik 2, 3, 4 Rohini, Mirgshira 1, 2	Mithun = **GEMINI** 61 – 90° Mirgshira 3, 4 Aruda Punarvasu 1, 2, 3	**3**
11	Kumb = **AQUARIUS** 301 – 330° Danishta, 3, 4 Satabisha Purva Bhadrapad 1, 2, 3		**Vedic Astrology and the twelve zodiac signs**	Kark = **CANCER** 91 – 120° Punarvasu · 4 Pushya, Ashlesha	**4**
10	Makar = **CAPRICORN** 271 – 300° Uttarashad 2, 3, 4 Sravana, Danishta 1, 2			Simha = **LEO** 121 – 150° Magha, Purva-Palguni Uttarapalguni-1	**5**
9	Danush = **SAGITTARIUS** 241 – 270° Moola, Purvashada Uttarashad-1	Virchak = **SCORPIO** 211 – 240° Vishaka-4, Anuradha Jeshta	Tula = **LIBRA** 181 – 210° Chitra 3, 4 Swati Vishaka-1, 2, 3	Kanya = **VIRGO** 151 – 180° Uttarapalguni 2,3, 4 Hasta, Chitra 1, 2	**6**
	8		**7**	

An expert astrologer can detect disturbing imbalances in a person's horoscope and thereby prescribe the best type of house and an auspicious time for building or buying. The positions of the various planets in a horoscope is crucial to many aspects of a person's life. In relation to one's house, the position of Mars, Venus, and Jupiter is especially important. And even more important is the planet a person has in the fourth house, as indicated in the following table:

Sun in the fourth house — a thatched roof home

Jupiter in the fourth house — a home of timber

Mercury in the fourth house — a regular building

Saturn in the fourth house — a home of concrete and steel

Venus in fourth house with other auspicious signs — a mansion.

Vastu, Astronomy, and Astrology

In Vedic astrology, if the following planets are auspiciously placed in one's horoscope they have a general influence and effect certain areas of one's office or home as follows:

The Sun benefits one's health and the worship conducted in a correctly positioned prayer room in the northeast or east

The Moon gives a positive mental disposition and benefits one's bathroom and drinking water with auspiciousness, and greatly enhances relationships in a correctly positioned guest room in the northwest

Mars provides powerful discipline energy (to both men and women) and bestows wealth and prosperity through correctly placed kitchens and open fires

Mercury enhances one's finances, business, and studies and positively influences a correctly positioned study and office in the north and a guest room in the northwest

Jupiter bestows respect, happiness, and expansion and protects money and valuable items when kept in the north and children's rooms when situated in the west and northeast

Venus endows eloquence and beauty (to both men and women) and auspiciously influences well placed living rooms in the east, west, north, and northwest and bedrooms in the west, south, and southwest

Saturn empowers one with discipline and bestows benefits upon a well placed dining room, animal shed, and pantry

Rahu in general generates inauspiciousness but protects a main entrance that is auspiciously situated in the north, northeast, or east.

Ketu in general invokes auspiciousness and bestows good fortune to a back entrance that is balanced with another entrance in the north or east. In a building with good Vastu, Rahu and Ketu protect the building on all sides.

Just as you are what you eat, you are also partially made up of the influences of Nature's immediate surroundings.

Vastu and Nature's Law of Karma

Vedic philosophy teaches that all universal activities and their reactions adhere to a universal law called karma. The Sanskrit word 'karma' means the activities of human beings. In the West, the law of karma is often misunderstood. The law of karma does not mean that one has no influence on fate and therefore one can act irresponsibly. On the contrary, the law of karma maintains that a human being is responsible for every single deed. Just as a misbehaved citizen under human laws loses his/her freedom, under the laws of Nature one is entrapped by one's own bad karmic reactions life after life and thereby loses freedom in various ways and to different degrees and in numerous species of life. As you sew, so shall you reap.

The symptoms of past good karma are health, wealth, education, and beauty whereas bad karma is characterised by disease, poverty, ignorance, and deformity. Harsh as it may seem, these are the facts of the cruel side of the laws of Nature, the subtle law of karma. What we do in this life with the scope of abilities we earned in our past lives determines the lifestyle we'll have now, and more importantly in our next life. We are the architects of our own future, and no one else is to blame. If one is currently ignorant of these principles it is because one was in a past life determined to forget higher principles and so Nature fulfils that desire of covering one's knowledge. Each individual is personally responsible for their own actions. At every moment we can choose to do good or bad. But for those who are fully enlightened, they can choose to go back to the spiritual sky and enjoy eternal freedom. All others simply choose to stay here in the material world and become entrapped again by the laws of karma. The choice is ours at every step. How we can create good karma and attain liberation to the spiritual world is clearly described in the greatest of all Vedic scriptures *Bhagavad–gita* and *Srimad-Bhagavatam*.

Human activities, therefore, are characterised by freedom and determination at every moment. None of us can detach ourselves from our previous activities which greatly influence our present situation. We must always remember that what we do now determines whether we move on to a better or worse situation in our next life. If we believe there is no next life, it all ends with this one, and if it turns out that this concept is wrong, and it has never been proved to be right, then the consequences are truly great. To the degree one's consciousness is spiritually developed, one can use his/her limited freedom to attain more freedom. At every moment we choose whether to live in harmony or disharmony with God's laws. We cannot blame God or anyone else if we get whammied for breaking Nature's laws. God is not harsh, His laws of Nature are harsh but then He warned us not to come here to the material world in the first place. But we ignored His loving plea. He never forces anyone to love Him, and here we are living with the laws of material existence against His wishes by our own choice. Therefore, the more we live in accordance with Nature's laws the more our freedom and happiness lasts, and the more we live in discord with Nature's laws the more we encounter misfortune.

The *Vedas* impart knowledge about the laws of Nature, the existence of God, and the ultimate purpose of life. Applying this knowledge enables us to

> The degree of happiness and distress one experiences in one's life is determined by Nature's law of karma. But each person decides for himself how to use this scope in order to design the future and develop consciousness.

> Mother Nature exhibits Her favour or anger, depending upon how we abide by her natural laws.

> *One's previous karma also determines whether or not one is born under the influence of an auspicious or inauspicious combination of planets, an influence that is also a major contributing factor in everything that one does now.*

The philosophy of the law of karma is one of responsibility, not irresponsibility. Even by the criteria of man made laws, the irresponsible are made to suffer and the responsible citizens are accordingly rewarded. God's law of karma is the same, but much more exacting. One's previous karma, therefore, is a major contributing factor in the success and failure of everything we do.

leave the cycle of karma and approach the eternal spiritual realm where life is unlimitedly perfect in every respect. The *Vedas* advise that while we are in this material world we should utilise the knowledge of *Vastu* to design our living space so that we can improve ourselves both materially and spiritually.

The living beings are regarded in the *Vedas* as spiritual entities who continually transmigrate in the material world from one body to a variety of others depending on their previous karma. In other words karma is an inescapable subtle law of Nature which rules that for every good or bad action given out one receives back an equally good or bad reaction either in this life or in a future life. What goes around comes around. Contrary to the idea that our happiness and distress come to us by accident, the *Vedas* teach that each one of us created our own current good or bad situation by the good and bad we created in past lives. Each individual was the past architect of his or her present situation and each individual now is the architect of his or her future life. The secrets of architecture lie deep within the Vedic scriptures. But in essence, the law of karma is a rule of fair play.

When the soul is completely disillusioned and frustrated with the numerous shortfalls of material experiences, he/she inquires about a deeper meaning to life. With the help of scripture and a self-realised liberated teacher, a lost soul can factually realise its eternal spiritual nature and swiftly return to the all blissful spiritual world. In this temporary material world, we cannot escape the miseries of birth, death, old age, and disease that Nature forces upon us according to our karma. In the spiritual world there is no bad karma and consequent suffering but rather everything is eternal, full of knowledge, and full of bliss.

The *Vedas* not only teach us the paths of liberation from the laws of karma in the material world but also how to live harmoniously with Nature in our own homes. Vedic knowledge of architecture, medicine, astronomy, music, martial arts, and so on are there to help us live peacefully and to gradually break free from the karmic cycle of birth and death in the material world. Adhering to the rules of *Vastu* while engaged in various material activities helps us transcend bad karma and thereby pursue spiritual elevation. In ancient India, worship of God and the powerful demigods was central to Vedic culture. Therefore, adhering to the rules of *Vastu* along with worshipping our divine origin undoubtedly frees us from the stringent karmic forces and sub-forces of the universe.

Vasati - the Modern Form of Vastu

"The demigods, being pleased by sacrifices, will also please you, and thus, by cooperation between men and demigods, prosperity will reign for all."
(Bhagavad-gita, 3.11)

Applying *Vastu* in our modern society is known as Vasati, which is derived from the word *Vastu*. In Sanskrit Vasati means 'healthy building'. This book, being the first of a series, contains the basics of *Vastu*/Vasati concepts. *Vastu* is an integral architectural concept. Since millennia, houses, temples, and even whole cities were built according to *Vastu*. Its basis are the natural laws of spatial energy, and this knowledge is used to bring the living space in resonance with Nature and its inhabitants. Your house is in fact the body of your body. Your house is also like a lens that focuses Nature's environmental influences. The quality of your living space influences your health as well as your mental and emotional status.

The old Indian geomancy system of *Vastu* has been scientifically shaped after millennia of experience and observation. With *Vastu* you can perceive Nature's subtle environmental influences on a person's health that arise from Earth´s magnetic field, the Earth and Suns' subtle energies, the paths of the Sun and the Moon, and gravitation. The combined influences define the quality of the living space in your office and home. The room is perceived as a bio-field that interacts with your own bio-energetic field. All these underlying interactions of Nature's laws are fully harmonised when building a house according to *Vastu*.

This book has covered the basics of the great science of *Vastu* that was first spoken by God himself when He spoke the *Vedas* at the time of the material creation many trillions of years ago. More rules apply to semi-detached houses (duplexes), terraced houses, housing estates, skyscrapers, penthouses, and so on. Additional differentiations are made according to the function and general character of a building. There are many additional regulations that influence the destiny of commercial buildings, hotels, restaurants, schools, educational institutions, and so on. All these and more will be covered in upcoming specialised *Vastu*/Vasati editions.

In order to fully comprehend and apply *Vastu*, we first need to acquaint ourselves with the basic philosophical understanding of the Vedic tradition of which *Vastu* forms an integral part. The *Vedas* regard man as part of a cosmic and divine order which can be understood by studying scripture, performing meditation, and subsequently acting according to scriptural directions.

The human race is undeniably under the inescapable influence of Nature which is made up of higher controlling living beings. This can only be fully understood and realised if we rise above our personal and national material egos and begin comprehending the bigger picture of cosmic and spiritual relationships. The *Vedas* state that as tiny humans on Earth it is simply foolish for us to conclude that we are completely independent of any higher control and that we can completely control Nature when in fact we are being constantly defeated. The *Vedas* state that rather than fight with Nature we should live in harmony, respecting all Nature's laws, and that such a peaceful co-existence is the best possible material attainment.

The *Vastu* scriptures teach that instead of acting against Nature we should first understand and then intimately and harmoniously connect ourselves with all of Nature's forces and creatively design our surrounding little worlds. Ancient

VASTU - The Origin of Feng Shui

Indian culture is famous for its colossal artistic temples which reflect the hierarchical aspect of our complex universe. The architecture of these temples is a unique bridge to higher beings and dimensions. We strive for freedom but it will always remain unattainable if we evade and even abuse Nature. The entire ecological system can only improve if we respect Nature by living in accordance with *Vastu*.

A Vasati consultant will consider which elements predominate or lack in both you and your buildings and then make balancing recommendations that encompass all your surrounding influences. If, for example, you personally are lacking in the fire element it would be recommended that you gain more exposure to the southeast and the balance of the fire element in southeast of your premises is sufficient or even slightly increased. A Vasati consultant is like a hot and cold mixer tap that enables you to get the temperature just right. If an already too fiery person has too much exposure to the southeast he/she will be extremely overheated with an unpredictable temperament. And if someone has both an insufficiency of the fire element in his/her person and dwelling there will be a lack lustre attribute in the personality.

Vedic architecture creates in our dwelling a reflection of the entire universe so that we can live in harmony with higher universal powers and influences. To the degree that one's dwelling conflicts with the cosmic structure the inhabitants will experience tensions and problems. In our surroundings we find both extremely positive and negative influences. An indiscriminate living structure cannot protect one from negative influences any more than a leaking roof can keep out the rain. Only buildings with the correct *Vastu* alignments can block Nature's multifarious energies and imbibe Her heavenly influences. Such architecture systematically projects the forces and aspects present in the cosmos onto the earth in a harmonious way. A living area is created which balances the problems of its inhabitants and gives positive access to both material and spiritual energies.

Sanskrit Glossary

Agni — The demigod of fire; the ruler of the South-east.

Brahma — The sub-creator of the universe and the original demigod.

Brahma-sthana — Geometrical and energetic centre point of a house or plot.

Chakras — subtle energy centres in the human body and a building.

Demigod — a powerful controller of a universal function residing in a heavenly planet.

Indra — the king of the demigods and ruler of the east.

Ketu — a shadow planet, sometimes represented by the tail of a dragon.

Kuvera — the demigod who controls wealth and is the ruler of the north.

Mandala — a symmetrical geometrical matrix directed towards a centre, illustrating or symbolising metaphysical relations in a graphical form.

Maya Danava — a disciple of Lord Brahma and founder of *Vastuvidya* which is prominent in North India.

Nairutva — a demon by nature but as powerful as a demigod and is the ruler of the southwest from where many inauspicious influences arise.

Om — a sound that precedes the chanting of most Vedic mantras and is said to contain the creative energies and powers of God.

Purusha — a powerful person being the enjoyer of Vedic sacrifices, as in the Vastu Purusha.

Putana — a demoniac female witch who is as powerful as a demigod and is also the ruler of the southwest from where many inauspicious influences arise.

Rahu — a shadow planet also sometimes represented by the head of a dragon.

Sanskrit — the original language of India, used to write the *Vedas*, said to be the mother of all languages, and spoken by the demigods.

Shilpin — a master of Vedic architecture.

Shiva — one of the most powerful demigods described in the *Vedas* as the great personality who periodically destroys the cosmos with a uniquely powerful dance.

Sthapati — a master of Vedic architecture.

Vastu — the Vedic science of building in harmony with Nature's multifarious influences.

Vastu Purusha — the lord who resides in all buildings and determines the quality of one's living space.

Vastu sastras — Vedic scriptures on the science of *Vastu*.

Vastuvidya — scientific knowledge that creates auspicious buildings.

Varuna — the demigod of the oceans and the ruler of the west.

Vayu — the demigod of the air and the ruler of the northwest.

Vedas — the ancient Sanskrit scriptures of India said to be God's instruction manuals for humankind to create peace and prosperity throughout the universe.

Vidya — knowledge.

Yamaraja — the demigod of death and ruler of the south.

Bibliography

In this first introductory book in English, I have referred to various books on *Vastu*. Some points have been drawn from original Sanskrit scriptures while others from academic classics. I have also referred to other modern works pertaining to the practical planning of a house. The following books were the most significant:

- *Vastushastra, An Edifice Science*, A.R. Tarkhedkar, Cosmo Publishing House, India, Dhulia 1995

- *Principles and Practice of Vastu Shastra*, V.V. Raman, Vidya Bhavan, Jaipur 1996

- *Vedic Architecture and Art of Living, A Book on Vastu Shastra*, B.B. Puri, Vastu Gyan Publication, Delhi 1995

- *Hidden Treasure of Vastu Shilpa Shastra and India Traditions*, Derebail Muralidhar Rao, SBS Publishers, Bangalore 1995

- *Srimad-Bhagavatam*, HDG A. C. Bhaktivedanta Swami Prabhupada

- *Vastu Shastra, Vol.1, Hindu Science of Architecture*, D.N. Shukla, Vastu-Vanmaya-Prakasana-Sala, Lucknow 1960

- *The Secret World of Vaasthu, Gouru Tirupati Reddy*, Prajahita Publishers, Hyderabad 1996

- *Vastu Sutra Upanishad*, A. Boner, Sadasiva Rath Sarma, Bettina Bäumer, Moltilal Banarsidass, Delhi

- *Bhagavad-gita As It Is*, HDG A. C. Bhaktivedanta Swami Prabhupada

- *Viswakarma Vastushastram*, K.V. Sastri, N.B. Gadre, Tanjore Sarasvati Mahal Series No. 85, Tanjore 1958

- *Matsya Purana - A Study*

- *The Matsya Purana*

- *Mosby-Year Book, Inc., 1993.Vitamin D from sunshine:* Wardlaw GM and Insel PM: Perspectives in Nutrition, Baltimore, MD.

About the Author

Marcus Schmieke, born in Oldenburg, Germany in 1966, has studied physics and philosophy in Hanover and Heidelberg. In 1989 he was initiated in a Vedic disciplic succession and spent many years in India studying Sanskrit, Vedic philosophy, and *Vastuvidya*. Since 1993, he has been working towards an integration of science and spirituality. He published his first articles on Vastu in the magazine *Tattva Viveka* which was co-founded by him in 1994. He is also the author of The Last Secret (1995) and The Living Field (1997), and published a conference booklet entitled Subtle Energies in Science and Medicine (1997). In 1996 he founded the Veda Academy for the integration of sciences and spirituality on Schloß Weißenstein, working on new paradigms in science and medicine as an interdisciplinary research and training institute.

In 1998 the Veda Academy expanded to Saxon, Switzerland, to increase Vedic research. Vastu forms an integral part of this work since Vedic architecture influences all aspects of life. In addition to his extensive study of all the original texts relating to Vastu, Marcus Schmieke solidified his technical knowledge of Vastu at the renowned South Indian Vastuvidyapratishanam Institute and was awarded a degree in Vastu. He is a master in Vastu and constantly gives seminars and trains students. He has written eight books on Vastu in German which have been translated into more than ten languages.

The Veda Academy in Germany

www.vedic-academy.com

Contacting a Vasati/Vastu Consultant

If you are interested in:

- house consultation
- correction tools: *Meru Chakra, Vasati Pyramid, Yantras, and more*
- books - CDs
- training seminars
- correspondence courses
- business consultation

Log on to:

www.mygoodvastu.com

UNITED KINGDOM

UK consultants:

Arthur Smith
P.O. Box 108
Watford, Herts. WD1 4SF
United Kingdom
Tel. & Fax: (+44) 01923-255108
E-mail: goloka@tesco.net
www.mygoodvastu.com

Sanjay Tanna
'Cintamani' Wall Hall Cottages
Aldenham, Herts WD2 8AS
United Kingdom
Tel: (+44) 01923-859365 Pager: (+44) 07623-188982
Email: mte@pamho.net
www.vasati.co.uk

USA

Mr. Thakur
Art & Culture Presentations, Inc.
PO Box 926337 Houston TX 77292
Tel 713 290 8715; Fax 713 290 8720
E-mail: thakurhari@aol.com

CANADA

Subramaniam Wichweswaran
992 Jean-Talon
Montreal, Quebec
Canada, H3N-1S8
Tel: (514) 278-4602
Fax: (514) 278-6030
wichwes@hotmail.com

GERMANY

Veden Academy
Marcus Schmieke
Hirschgrund 94
01814 Schöna
Germany
Tel. (+49) 035028-80088 Fax (+49) 035028-80089
Email: Marcus.Schmieke@T-Online.de
www.vasati.de (English and German)

Visit **www.vedic-academy.com** and experience online a virtual Vedic college in English and German. Enroll for a course on Vasati (Vastu for the modern world), Vedic Astrology, Vedic Philosophy, Vedic Spirituality, Science and Spirituality, Sanskrit, Ayurveda, Bharata Natyam, and many other topics. Courses are either private or collective.

Reviews:

"I wanted to buy a new house and I commissioned Arthur Smith to check out a newly built housing development. He steered me away from a house with negative features and directed me to a house with good Vastu. I additionally installed a Meru Chakra and am now enjoying a harmonious living space I have never experienced before." James Fenton, UK.

"I read the book on Vastu and invited Arthur Smith to do a consultation for my new family home. He confirmed that my plot has a very auspicious shape and slope with panoramic views in the best place. He drew up plans for my home based entirely upon Vastu, showing how to get the maximum auspiciousness from Nature." Hema Gauri, Spain.

"Two weeks after installing a Meru Chakra in my house I got the IT job I always wanted. It was incredible. The Meru Chakra definitiely brings in good fortune." Minesh Pujara, UK.

"While Arthur Smith was installing a Meru Chakra in my house, some unexpeceted money arrived in the post. Ever since then, many auspicious things have been happening, particularly with my house. I now have a better and new house." Susan Bell, UK.

"The Vastu in my house is not so good, but not too bad either. I had a Vasati Pyramid installed and immediately noticed that the energies in my home were different, much more tranquil. I had a Meru Chakra installed and the next day I won a very valuable new business contract. A month later I installed another Meru Chakra in my other apartment and the next day I won another big and lucrative overseas business contract. I'm glad I got a Meru Chakra." H. Bolton, UK.

childrens bedroom, study, living room, storage, and dining room	free space for the auspicious (N) inside positioning ether element	main entrance, reception room, study/office, bathroom, and basement below	adults bedroom, heavy storage, and recreation	dining room, staircase, bedroom, and heavy storage	kitchen, central heating, and electircal equipment	reception room, study, guest r… childrens bedr… and toilet in north/northwe…
adults bedroom, heavy storage, and recreation	dining room, staircase, bedroom, and heavy storage	kitchen, central heating, and electircal equipment	reception room, study, guest room, childrens bedroom, and toilet in north/northwest	main entrance, office/study, basement below, valuables storage, and reception hall/lounge	prayer/meditatiion, basement below, living room, and children's bedroom	childrens bedr… study, living ro… storage, and dining room
reception room, study, guest room, childrens bedroom, and toilet in north/northwest	main entrance, office/study, basement below, valuables storage, and reception hall/lounge	prayer/meditatiion, basement below, living room, and children's bedroom	childrens bedroom, study, living room, storage, and dining room	free space for the auspicious (N) inside positioning ether element	main entrance, reception room, study/office, bathroom, and basement below	adults bedroo… heavy storage and recreation
childrens bedroom, study, living room, storage, and dining room	free space for the auspicious (N) inside positioning ether element	main entrance, reception room, study/office, bathroom, and basement below	adults bedroom, heavy storage, and recreation	dining room, staircase, bedroom, and heavy storage	kitchen, central heating, and electircal equipment	reception room, study, guest r… childrens bedr… and toilet in north/northwe…
adults bedroom, heavy storage, and recreation	dining room, staircase, bedroom, and heavy storage	kitchen, central heating, and electircal equipment	reception room, study, guest room, childrens bedroom, and toilet in north/northwest	main entrance, office/study, basement below, valuables storage, and reception hall/lounge	prayer/meditatiion, basement below, living room, and children's bedroom	childrens bedr… study, living r… storage, and dining room
reception room, study, guest room, childrens bedroom, and toilet in north/northwest	main entrance, office/study, basement below, valuables storage, and reception hall/lounge	prayer/meditatiion, basement below, living room, and children's bedroom	childrens bedroom, study, living room, storage, and dining room	free space for the auspicious (N) inside positioning ether element	main entrance, reception room, study/office, bathroom, and basement below	adults bedroo… heavy storage and recreatio…
childrens bedroom, study, living room, storage, and dining room	free space for the auspicious (N) inside positioning ether element	main entrance, reception room, study/office, bathroom, and basement below	adults bedroom, heavy storage, and recreation	dining room, staircase, bedroom, and heavy storage	kitchen, central heating, and electircal equipment	reception roo… study, guest… childrens bed… and toilet in north/northw…
adults bedroom, heavy storage, and recreation	dining room, staircase, bedroom, and heavy storage	kitchen, central heating, and electircal equipment	reception room, study, guest room, childrens bedroom, and toilet in north/northwest	main entrance, office/study, basement below, valuables storage, and reception hall/lounge	prayer/meditatiion, basement below, living room, and children's bedroom	childrens bed… study, living r… storage, and dining room
reception room, study, guest room, childrens bedroom, and toilet in north/northwest	main entrance, office/study, basement below, valuables storage, and reception hall/lounge	prayer/meditatiion, basement below, living room, and children's bedroom	childrens bedroom, study, living room, storage, and dining room	free space for the auspicious (N) inside positioning ether element	main entrance, reception room, study/office, bathroom, and basement below	adults bedro… heavy storag… and recreatio…